The
Opposite of
Everything
Is True

The Opposite of Everything Is True

Reflections on Denial in Alcoholic Families

William H. Crisman, M.Div., S.T.M.

William Morrow and Company, Inc.　New York

8-26-97

Credo from *All I Really Need to Know I Learned in Kindergarten* by Robert Fulghum. Copyright © 1986, 1988 by Robert Fulghum. Reprinted by permission of Villard Books, a division of Random House, Inc.

Diagram and explanation of the "Mosaic Theory of the Etiology of Alcoholism and Other Chemical Dependence" from *Alcoholism, Attachments, and Spirituality: A Transpersonal Approach* by Charles L. Whitfield. Used by permission of the author.

Jellnick chart reprinted by permission of Charter Hospitals of Louisville.

The Twelve Steps are reprinted with permission of Alcoholics Anonymous World Services, Incorporated. Permission to reprint The Twelve Steps does not mean that AA has reviewed or approved the contents of this publication, nor that AA agrees with the views expressed herein. AA is a program of recovery for alcoholism. Use of The Twelve Steps in connection with programs and activities which are patterned after AA but which address other problems does not imply otherwise.

Recognizing the importance of preserving what has been written, it is the policy of William Morrow and Company, Inc., and its imprints and affiliates to have the books it publishes printed on acid-free paper, and we exert our best efforts to that end.

Library of Congress Cataloging-in-Publication Data

Crisman, William H.
    The opposite of everything is true / William H. Crisman.
      p.   cm.
    ISBN 0-688-09179-2
    ISBN 0-688-10420-7 (pbk.)
      1. Alcoholics—Rehabilitation—United States.   2. Alcoholics—
United States—Family relationships.   3. Denial (Psychology)
I. Title.
HV5279.C75   1989
362.29'28—dc20   90-6427
                                                    CIP

Printed in the United States of America

First Edition

1 2 3 4 5 6 7 8 9 10

BOOK DESIGN BY KATHRYN PARISE

To Howard, Peter, Gregory, Raymond, and Alva.
We get what we need, and sometimes what we want.
In the place of the first, my father who died too soon,
I have been gifted with four guides—good, wise,
and (thank God!) very, very human men.

Acknowledgments

With gratitude, I wish to mention those this book and I have had to depend upon so totally:

Bill Dare, who had the wonderful gall to submit my name to a publisher as a possible author without telling me about it.

Boyd Griffin of Hearst Publishing, who took my suggestion seriously; but who had to write me twice to get me to take his invitation to write with equal seriousness.

Clarke Evans, for editing, countless good suggestions, and friendship; and Rachael Wright, for word processing and endless patience. The gift of their support amazes me even more today at the end than it did in the beginning.

My Twelve-Step communities, especially Alva L., Trish D., Tom W., and Andy E. They have given me my recovery and my life.

My AA sponsees and my clients, who in their determination to heal and their willingness to trust are my teachers and my inspiration.

Dr. Keith Smith and his staff at Tacoma Chiropractic Clinic, whose skill and support kept an aching spine and protesting arm adjusted and supple enough to stay to the task at hand.

Liza Dawson, senior editor at William Morrow and Company, who knew how to suggest insightfully enough (and goad tactfully enough) that it all got done—on time, no less.

Father Jim Dunning, from whose "File 29B" I got the title of this book and other accumulated bits of flotsam.

And Victoria, who always knew it would happen.

Contents

Introduction

When I'm the speaker at an AA meeting, I introduce myself like this: "My name is Bill. I'm an alcoholic and addict. I'm the grandson of an alcoholic, the stepson of a compulsive gambler, and I'm a codependent. Today, I do counseling with people in recovery, and I teach. I was a Catholic priest for seventeen years, and for the twelve years before that I was a seminarian studying for priesthood. I've been in recovery just over nine years—one day at a time."

In Twelve-Step terminology, those sentences give the bare-bones outline of my "Qualification," my proof that I stand before them not by reason of their invitation or tolerance but by right. I've paid my dues—and because of that, as well as my continuing desire not to drink or use, I have the right to share my story and find belonging in the Fellowship. They, in turn, welcome me because I am one of them—not in spite of what I've been but because of it.

The stories we share at meetings are often amazing—extraordinary accounts of extraordinarily distorted ventures into the extremes of human behavior and feeling. But there is an axiom each of us soon discovers as we wind our ways into recovery: "The more extraordinary the story, the more ordinary the drunk."

This book contains some extraordinary stories, yet telling the "amazing" is not my primary focus or my purpose in writing it. Rather, the surprising and tragic fact is that the themes we'll explore in these pages are the normal and the ordinary plot lines of the lives of at least 50 percent of our population. The conservative estimate is that 10 percent of the people of our country are alcoholic, and that each alcoholic directly affects the lives of at least five other people. It's no great feat to work out the mathematics of the situation. And note: We haven't even begun to deal with those enmeshed in other forms of chemical dependency.

In that sense, I find my life to be an ordinary variation on the life themes played out by all chemical dependents. My dependency has been less dramatic than many—fairly average in its development and length, but just as devastating as anyone else's. So, too, is my recovery ordinary: I've progressed through the stages of healing in predictable ways and according to the normal time schedule.

From the time I was nineteen until I was thirty-eight, the continuing, daily, ordinary, unifying thread to my life was chemical dependency. Those nineteen years began with a psychiatrist's prescription for Valium and petered out on the dregs of a vodka bottle. I did not end up on Skid Road (although, God knows, I got far closer to it than I want to admit). I didn't do roaring binges; I never got a DWI (Driving While Intoxicated). I functioned, usually with competence, sometimes with excellence. Many of my closest associates and friends were surprised and disbelieving when they found out I'd gone to treatment. I was trustworthy and worked hard.

But I was and am a drunk. My experience tells me Skid Road is as much an inner state as it is a concrete place; that the DWIs I deserved but didn't get are as real as actual, police-issued tickets; that a life lived solely for the appreciation and approval of others is as empty as one wasted on the streets; and that the inability to not drink can be just as real for the gentleman (or priest) with his brandy as it is for the bum with his rotgut.

The majority of my drinking and drugging I do not remember, precisely because it was such an ordinary, daily aspect of my life. I seldom, very seldom, got drunk in the common sense of the word. Instead, I used only enough—day in and day out—to get to a level of emotional smoothness that allowed me to function and perform in the ways I was supposed to. Starkly put, I could not do my life without my chemicals. In the treatment trade, that's called "maintenance drinking."

Consequently, I don't have many drinking stories to share with you. My times of greatest desperation and most aberrant behavior have to do with the occasions when I ran out of Valium or alcohol and would do anything to get resupplied—such as driving sixty miles at three o'clock in the morning to get the pill bottle I'd forgotten to pack before a class outing in the mountains.

What I came to know with dreaded familiarity, though, is the inner stuff of chemical dependency—the feelings of isolation and emptiness, the cynicism of drained and empty dreams, the slowly increasing paranoia, the quietly corrosive resentments, the compulsive need to be right, the unspoken but oh-so-real realization of being trapped and enslaved, and most of all the growing fear that I was going insane.

In recovery—slowly but steadily—all that has changed. And that change is what this book is about. Although I can sketch the outline of that change and describe its process, although I can tell you what happened, I have to admit I cannot tell you why it happened. The people, the events, the circumstances are clear; but why they have all come together as they have is a mystery.

In the midst of the mystery, though, one fact has become intensely clear. My chemical dependency is not just mine alone. I, like every alcoholic and addict, stand within a context of family, society, and culture. Those contexts condition, form, and mold us in both genetic and environmental ways; they cannot be denied.

I have come to believe we can ignore those contexts only at the risk of our recoveries and, consequently, our very lives. Thus, in order to tell my story, or the story of any chemical dependent, I need to expand my focus to see how I fit in. For I *do* fit in, I do have a place. I may be a discordant note in the symphony, but the performance would be incomplete without me.

So the stories I share will be not only about us addicts and alcoholics but about our families and our society as well. Together, and only together, we make coherent sense; apart we do not.

I hope as I paint the wider picture, you'll be able to find a place in it for yourself. For I presume nobody picks up a book subtitled *Reflections on Denial in Alcoholic Families* by accident. I'm guessing that you're investigating what I have to say because you have your own personal acquaintance with the Wonderland of addiction and dysfunction—and that you want to find a way out.

If this book can be of help, great, but please be aware of a few points from the beginning. First, this is not a self-help, "How-to-Do-It" book. I doubt that anyone could write such a book or devise such a program. The issues are so deep and each person is so individual that I view any person, book, or program that claims to know "The" way to recovery with intense suspicion.

Second, even though I speak from a perspective of hope, and believe passionately in the hope of which I speak, I must note that recovery happens only for a small minority of chemical dependents and their families. I've heard the figure bandied about that only 13 percent or so of practicing addicts and alcoholics make it into any sort of recovery program, including Twelve-Step programs. Of that 13 percent, only about 5 percent make it to five years of chemical sobriety. I hope these figures are too pessimistic; but my own experience, as well as that of many chemical-dependency professionals with whom I've spoken, tends to confirm them.

Last, therefore, what I hope you might get from what follows is a "sense," a "taste," a "smell" for where the real issues lie. Most of all, I hope you get a "feel" about denial. In one way or another, everything we'll explore has to do with denial. If you were to compare the lives of chemical dependents and their families to rivers, denial would be the riverbeds through which all that craziness, pain, stress, abuse, and self-destruction flow. So much is that so that I'm willing to flatly and absolutely assert that without denial you can't have alcoholics or addicts, or the insanity in which the members of their families live. Consequently, if you develop a nose for denial, you have a chance of confronting this issue head-on. You have a chance of discovering the true enemy beneath all its disguises—a chance to pin the right tail on the right donkey. And you'll know why I entitled this book *The Opposite of Everything Is True.*

I can't give you a good reason why you *should* read this book. I'd certainly like you to—and so would my bookkeeper—but there's really no necessity for you to investigate what I've got to say. If you accept my invitation, however, I think you'll find that what follows is not just a rehash of other authors' work. They've spent a lot of time investigating the ins and outs of chemical dependency and its effects on family members—its origins, development, and consequences.

I esteem their work and find it an invaluable resource in my practice. Books like Claudia Black's *It Will Never Happen to Me,*[1] Melody Beattie's *Codependent No More,*[2] and Charles Whitfield's *Healing the Child Within*[3] have helped many of my clients to get a handle on what's happening in their lives. I've no need to repeat what they've already said.

I write from the viewpoint of one who's been there. That fact in no way assures me of having all the answers. But it does give me an authority like that a war veteran enjoys: When we tell of our battles, we don't speak from theory; we've got the scars to validate what we say.

So, if you'd like a bird's-eye view of the battlefield plus some sense of how this war came to be in the first place, come along. Let's explore together. I believe that, despite the confusion, pain, and wreckage of the past, we can uncover foundation stones for life and hope in days to come.

[1] Claudia Black, *It Will Never Happen to Me* (New York: Ballantine/Self Help, 1981).
[2] Melody Beattie, *Codependent No More* (New York: Harper/Hazelden, 1987).
[3] Charles Whitfield, *Healing the Child Within* (Deerfield Beach, FL: Health Communications, 1987).

Part One

"The Bad News"

Chapter 1

Setting the Scene

An Introduction to Addiction, Dependency, and Denial
Personal Reflections on Their Depth and Power

In 1973 and 1974, I was doing doctoral studies in theology at the Institute of Christian Thought in Toronto. Due to my Valium addiction, I never completed the doctorate.

Finished or not, however, those studies have fascinated me ever since, especially in my area of specialization, the dynamics of conversion. In its most basic terms, conversion is the process one goes through while moving from one system of belief to another. For example, if a man is raised a conservative Republican but finds himself, through the unique process of his own life, becoming a Democrat or a Socialist, he has undergone a conversion. Or if a woman changes her religious value system and becomes a Protestant after being raised a Catholic, she has converted.

It may seem a long jump from the detached study of academic theology to the agonizing world of suicidal alcoholism, Alcoholics Anonymous (AA), and recovery. But, if I'm to believe the witness of my own life—my addiction and alcoholism, and my recovery; and if I'm to believe the witness of the people with whom I work— their illness and their healing; the jump is really very short.

For—I'm convinced—to be able to move from the practice of one's alcoholism and addiction into recovery entails nothing less than a conversion as deep and heart-moving as any a religious faith could demand or expect. As the advertising pamphlet of a treatment center puts it, "Recovery—a transforming experience."

Alcoholism/addiction (chemical dependency) is a slippery thing. Every time someone comes up with a definition for it, someone else dreams up an exception to that definition. It involves drinking and using, yet anyone from the AA or Narcotics Anonymous (NA) tables will tell you that drinking and using are only symptoms of the "disease"—and not even necessary ones. Clancy I., a well-known AA speaker from southern California, runs a mission for skid-road alcoholics in Los Angeles. He tells stories of holding many of them in his arms as they die from their alcoholism. And as they die, they protest, "It wasn't the booze. . . ." And he replies, "I know."

Most recovering chemical dependents today do not see themselves as evil persons; rather, they are sick. And we who work professionally in the field of recovery build the body of our work on the conviction that we deal with disease, not moral degeneration. Yet anyone in recovery will tell you that one of the essential ingredients of healing is to do an exhaustive inventory of the immoralities one committed while drinking and using.

The paradoxes—or contradictions, if you wish—go on and on. And if that is so for addicts and alcoholics directly, even more is it true for those whose lives they touch—especially the members of their families.

Ask spouses or lovers of alcoholics why they got involved with their alcoholics in the first place, much less stayed with and endured that chemically dependent behavior over the years, and the answer will be, "Out of love." In the name of love, spouses and friends of alcoholics become "codependents." They manipulate, enable, and control—looking for, hoping for, expecting changes and healing. Yet throughout almost the whole of their lives with their alcoholics/addicts, the overwhelming weight of evidence says it's stupid to expect any change: The "disease" marches on, and alcoholics/addicts just keep getting worse until they die. Nevertheless, codependents still believe, "If we only love them long enough and strongly enough, they will change."

To Adult Children of Alcoholics (ACOAs), the contradictions can become almost mockingly cruel. There's not one of us who doesn't long for some relationship, some human connection, to fill the empty spaces and the open wounds of childhood abandonment and abuse. But God help us if we ever say, "I love you," to another; for then the war is on. The closer we get to our beloved, the more defensed, fearful, rigid, and battering our attitudes and mind-sets become. Love means intimacy and vulnerability, but our childhoods told us that intimacy begot abandonment and that vulnerability's partner was abuse; so the closer we get in our loving, the more we expect the battering to begin once again.

In short, to paraphrase the "Big Book" of Alcoholics Anonymous, chemical dependency is "cunning, baffling, and powerful"—for the chemical dependents, certainly, but equally for their spouses in their codependency and their children in their paradependency as well. Life in the chemically dependent family is a game of "denial," played with mirrors, where the opposite of everything is true and the only guaranteed reality is that what we see and what we want is *not* what we get.

Only when we comprehend denial—its pervasiveness, its power, and its tenacity—will the contradictions of chemical dependency's "Wonderland" resolve themselves into some kind of coherence. That is why this pervasive denial is my focal point.

"The identifying symptom of alcoholism/addiction is denial." That's a commonplace around the AA tables, as well as the universal experience of anyone who tries to deal with alcoholics and addicts. Chemical dependency is a disease that tells its victims they're not sick; all they know is that they hurt. Every time I tried to stop drinking on my own, I felt I was going to die. I'm talking here not just about a morning-after hangover; physical pain was only a small part of it. I'm referring to an all-embracing, emotional, spiritual, and physical sense of shattering emptiness, agitation, confusion, and brokenness. It was utterly terrifying, and I had no doubt that my life was over. So I did what any self-respecting person does when he comes face-to-face with a life-endangering threat. I ran—right back to what made me feel like I was alive once again, my drugs and alcohol. (If you've been there, you know what I mean; if you haven't, you can only guess.)

Quite a while before I quit drinking and drugging, my head told me that the chemicals were killing me. I rationally understood that objective truth. But my far more profound level of perception—my gut—told me that I had to have them or I'd die. I believed my gut. Intuitively, I knew I had to use what little energies I had left to get it over with quickly—commit suicide; or go someplace where nothing else would intrude on my drinking—Skid Road.

All of that wasn't necessarily conscious or thought out, but on that core level of intuition and adrenaline that guards our very survival, it seemed obvious and was completely persuasive. My life was disintegrating around me, but my use of alcohol and drugs was not, could not be, why. I didn't have a problem there.

Note the paradox. In plain fact, the use of booze and drugs was killing me; or rather, I was killing myself in slow motion by using them. And even though I could *rationally* see that fact, I could not believe it because my gut told me that my survival depended on continuing to use the stuff. And the more dependent I became, the more I believed my gut.

As a survivor, Robinson Crusoe had nothing on me. I've always done anything and everything I perceived I needed to do to keep breathing, even if it meant believing that black is white, or life is death and death is life. I conned a doctor friend into supplying me with Valium, convincing him as I had convinced myself that I was taking the drug "as prescribed." I manipulated my society of priests to transfer me from my doctoral work to a seminary assignment because I—with my particular skills—was "needed" there; not because my addiction had so debilitated me that I couldn't even write a whole sentence. Anything to protect my secret and my need . . .

By the end of my drinking and using, *based on results,* my life was actually about dying; yet I believed, with ever-deepening desperation, that everything I did, especially my drinking, was about staying alive. So, to stay alive (i.e., to drink) I stole and lied and cheated and betrayed—with every sense of righteousness.

People Who Love People

Even at my worst, I wasn't alone. I've always had people who love me, and they did what loving people do: They stood by me, getting more and more concerned. But, as for me, so for them: It was a downward, swirling vortex. The sicker I got, the more concerned they became; and consequently, the more of their emotional horizons I filled, the more emotional power they gave me. As I got sicker, they got more agitated and despairing (and sucked in).

And because they loved me, they believed me. When I told them I didn't have a problem with drugs or alcohol, they accepted my word. Besides, I was a maintenance drinker (that is, I drank just enough each day to get to a level of feeling good enough to function); I did not get drunk (thank you very much). In fact, I drove the drunk ones home! Of course, what other people didn't see was how much or how often I drank when I was alone, and so their perceptions corroborated my word. Even though they could see and experience the disintegration of my life, they, like me, believed I did not have a problem with chemicals. It had to be something else.

Add one final layer to their confusion and pain. Because of their own personal experiences with drunkenness in their families and neighbors, because of our pervasive societal revulsion with drunkenness, the last thing in the world they wanted me to be was a drunk. I could be emotionally ill, or stupid, or even criminal—anything but a drunk.

Put it all together, and the conclusion is both devastating and unavoidable. Because the people who loved me did love me, and did believe me, and did believe their own perceptions, and did not want me to be a drunk, to them my drinking and drugging were not and could not be my real problem. Just like me, they ended up living in habitual denial. It was very confusing and very crazy.

I'm unique, but the story of my addictiveness isn't. The outline is the same for every chemical dependent, and for all who love and associate with them: In order to survive (and always in the name of love), denial is the name of the game. "If you don't (can't) see my problem, I won't see yours. . . ." Take our present "war on drugs," for example: Our leaders demand the death penalty for crack and cocaine dealers and harsh sentences for users; yet as a society, we legitimize nearly unlimited access to alcohol, the deadliest drug of all.

Thus, my alcoholism was never just my own. No matter how successfully I hid my drinking and using, the denial it ingrained into me had an inevitable impact on the emotional lives of those who loved me. In a relatively short time, actually, my alcoholism became the basis of an entire social *system* of denial whose entire purpose and goal was to enable me to escape the truth. It's no exaggeration to say that those denial patterns in me, in my family, and in my friends were a living, growing commitment to insanity. More and more, the opposite of everything—for me, for them—became the truth.

From that personal experience, and from the like experiences of alcoholic after alcoholic, I'm led to contend that what began as "a lie here and an avoidance there" soon became for me an ingrained, personal habit of denial. And then, in the same way, the same thing happened to my family and friends. What's more, those denial systems (mine and theirs) depended upon each other and mutually reinforced each other. The longer it went on, the deeper, stronger, and more encompassing the process became; the more it seemed to assume a life of its own; the more it took to itself our ability to act, our power.

What Denial?

From all of that, let's draw some conclusions. Denial is a social thing—a social disease, if you wish. It is dynamic, constantly drawing energy to itself to buttress itself and expand its hold. And in a very short time, it becomes the lens through which all the awareness, feelings, and behaviors of its subjects are filtered. For example, the presence of a migraine headache can make it seem that every child within hearing is screaming at the top of his lungs, that every unexpected turn of events is a catastrophe, that every question is an attack on your personality. If you always have a migraine, life is always a bitch.

It is no great news to observe that we human beings spend most of our time for most of our days engaged in practical affairs of life. And most of those "practical affairs of life" have to do with survival. I work hard so my pets and I can be warm and healthy. You raise your kids—see to their education and values—so they'll have a decent chance at life when they grow up. We all vote and participate in politics so we can preserve and strengthen our way of life. We tax ourselves to provide health care for the unfortunate and to set up criminal-justice systems to protect ourselves and the ones we love.

That is what people see us doing, that is what we see ourselves doing when we stop to take a look. We do what we need to do so that our lives have a chance to work. On a daily basis, then, making our lives work is what it's all about.

But the question is, "How do we know what makes our lives work and what doesn't?" I'd suggest that we are guided by a kind of distilled wisdom, drawn from experience and trial and error. If we scorch our fingers on the stove, we stop touching heated burners. If a coworker gossips about a secret we've shared with him, we get careful—very careful—about those we talk to in the future. Or, again, either I do my work in the way that pleases my boss or I get fired. We find out that if we do this and that, we survive, we get what we want out of life; and if we don't do these things in the correct order, we don't achieve our goals—we don't survive.

All of that seems obvious, I suppose. But the really fascinating thing about the process of making our lives work is that *it's so obvious, we don't even think about it.* We just do it habitually, nonreflectively. We develop, as it were, a "habitual groove" of consciousness, feeling, and behavior—a channeled pattern of living that holds our lives together and makes them work.

Nine times out of ten, that "wisdom," that common sense, works. But when denial enters onto the scene, common sense and wisdom are suddenly up for grabs. I can believe I'm surviving and getting my life to work when, in fact, I'm actually losing my grip day by day and heading on a beeline for self-destruction.

I can believe—based on my latest raise and my boss's pleasure with my work—that I'm furthering myself and succeeding at my career, while the truth is that I've stressed myself into ulcers and burnout, neglected my kids, and effectively abandoned my spouse. Or, as actually happened, I could see myself as a success in the parish because my pastor (who had a bit of a drinking problem himself) praised my ability to ". . . drink with men, and gain their respect."

What happens if the truth is the exact opposite of what I perceive and understand it to be? What if other people—important, authoritative people—not only do not challenge how I see my reality but in fact support my view and interpretation of what's going on—and do so because they believe in my understanding as much as I do? The opposite of everything suddenly comes true.

In the Beginning . . .

Let me illustrate how that system of denial develops with some stories from my own life.

In my first year of graduate school, my inner world began to fall apart. (How that came to be I'll leave to a future chapter.) It was one of those times when there are no answers, and the pit of my stomach seemed to drag along the bottom of the Grand Canyon. My seminary adviser didn't know how to confront my trauma, so he sent me to a psychiatrist. The psychiatrist, I'm sure, thought he had a potential suicide on his hands, so he prescribed what he called his "cocktail" to get me back to some sort of equilibrium. The cocktail's recipe was potent: an "upper," a "downer," and Valium to level them out. After six months or so, he took me off the upper and downer, but left me on the Valium with the words, "If I can't trust somebody who's going to be a priest, who can I trust?" Who was I to resist a manipulation like that?

Two years before I hit bottom, I consulted with the archbishop of Seattle about some of my personal difficulties. Raymond Hunthausen didn't become archbishop by being naive. He put two and two together and asked me if I had any trouble with alcohol. I answered no, and I believed my answer.

That I believed I was telling him the truth is the crux of the matter. I genuinely believed that even though I had some "difficulties," overall my life was working. If he had questioned me about my pre-supper cocktails or before-bed brandies, I probably could have passed a lie-detector test as I argued that my use of alcohol actually helped make my life work. It relaxed me and made me more convivial; it smoothed my tensions and helped me socialize.

Not long after that, on the Fourth of July, 1977, I had a break in tolerance. I thought I was experiencing a depressive breakdown. So, I called a friend, who took me to the hospital. My skin got clammy, my insides started to shake, my stomach felt as though it were in free-fall, and I started to cry uncontrollably. The emergency staff called in a psychiatrist. He asked me what was going on. I diagnosed myself as severely depressed, and he agreed. We did a year's worth of therapy together after that, with nothing being said about my drinking other than that I should keep my intake "moderate."

I could multiply the examples (and will later on), but enough of them for now. The two I've offered get to the core of the problem. For, you see, in spite of the "difficulties" I reported to the archbishop, in spite of the ensuing breakdown, *I still continued to function*. Whatever my troubles, to those around me (and to myself) my life still seemed to work. I was a priest; I did the things priests do very well. As long as I did those things, neither I nor those who observed me could grasp that my insides were disintegrating. The fact was that the more I was falling apart on the inside, the better I did on the outside. Paradoxically, the very actions that in a healthy life should be the measures of success had become for me the pillars of my denial. I really did believe myself when I told the archbishop I had no problem with booze. Had he pressed the point, I would have proven it to him.

Archbishop Hunthausen, though, was probably the only person in my life who saw the forest for the trees. At least, he was the only one who had insight enough to pinpoint what was going on and the courage to tell me what he suspected. But there was no way I could hear him. My belief was stronger than his insight. Over the years, the props I'd put in place to shore up and defend my style of living were still too firm to be shaken, either by my difficulties or by his intuition.

River Deep . . .

It's hard to explain to someone who's not "been there" how my belief—my denial—could be so powerful and all-enveloping that it blinded me to my own truth. A comparison will help.

My daily routine—getting up, saying mass, doing my work, taking my Valium or drinking my cocktails—was the "surface stuff," the flowing water. What I didn't (wouldn't), (couldn't) see was the riverbed beneath, that deep channel of denial through which it all coursed and by which it was guided. My life all seemed to fit together; it seemed to work, for me and for others.

The deeper the habit pattern—the groove—the more likely a life will continue moving along the course it has already been following. We spend our energies, usually and habitually, enlarging upon and developing the "groove" through which we already "flow," unconcerned with finding a new "riverbed" for the ongoing stream of our lives.

What seemed like a life of fulfillment and success was, in fact, nothing but a well-oiled mechanism that enabled me to get on with my personal version of slow-motion suicide.

If you had stood alongside my life, looking at its surface currents and eddies, you would have seen what I saw—its accomplishments, its effectiveness for other people, its externals. You would not have seen the slow-motion erosion and disintegration happening down below, within me. For the most part, you wouldn't even have been able to see my drinking. I did it in secret, and very, very seldom to the point of actual drunkenness. And like you, I couldn't see the depths, either, because I was numbing myself on a daily basis, anesthetizing myself to the pain with Valium, Scotch, and brandy.

And so it went for close to twenty-three years. I got ordained, taught in three seminaries, earned two master's degrees, and worked well (judging by the feedback) in a number of parishes. Judging by the surface stuff, I was a success. The longer I practiced my chemical dependency, the more habitual it became, the more I became (like the river in its channel) grooved into it. Only a major catastrophe would have been able to disrupt that guiding pattern of my life.

But you can't tell a river's eventual goal by standing on its bank watching it flow by. It may eventually empty into the Gulf of Mexico, a thousand miles to the south. Yet where you stand beside it, admiring its sparkling surface, it may be coursing west to get around a range of mountains. You can only see what you can see.

Only one person stood up above, on the canyon's rim, to see where my life would eventually go—and his voice wasn't strong enough to be heard. The canyon was too deep and the river's roar too loud.

So, Who Am I?

An inescapable fact of our lives is mutuality; we are not alone in this life. We are born into families, and our families live within wider societies and cultures. This belonging to families and societies is not a superficial, accidental reality. The brute fact is that if they don't exist, I don't exist. No matter how strong and independent an individual I may be, I didn't get born by myself; I didn't dream up my language by myself; I didn't develop my taste in food by myself. I depend inevitably, necessarily, absolutely on you—and you on me.

That is true for my belief system and for yours: I simply cannot "have" myself, or even my beliefs about myself and what my life is about, without you. But neither can you "have" yourself and your beliefs without me.

So, then, our belief systems are mutual and interdependent. They are, in the normal course of our lives, the all-powerful channels guiding the flow of our decisions and behaviors. They consume and define the major energies of our day-to-day existence. They possess the overarching, directing theme that gives us purpose and meaning.

All that has been described above applies to every person, healthy or unhealthy. So, to find out what anybody is about, we have to uncover and study the riverbed of his or her belief system. That's ticklish—for two reasons.

1. When you and I meet each other, "what" we meet is our physical presences, our behaviors, and our impressions of each other's thoughts and feelings. We do not walk about with billboards listing our beliefs or with menus of our behaviors and habits. In truth, we probably couldn't tell one another what the guiding beliefs and habits of our lives are, even if we wanted to. Unless we take the time to study the flow of our lives, most of us—most of the time—are simply unaware of what guides us. We are so caught up in the business of day-to-day living and surviving that we don't or can't take the time to assess the overall flow of our existence. We see and experience the surface and not much else.

2. Very few of us, especially in today's scattered society, have the chance to spend our whole lives with another person. We meet, we spend some time, then we pass along. To employ our analogy of a river once again: If I stand on the bank, even camp there for a month, and only experience the water flowing west, how could I possibly know that fifty miles downstream it takes a bend around a mountain range to resume its ultimate direction—to the south? It is just not often that we get a chance to view the overall landscape, either of our own lives or of someone else's. To do that, I would need time to walk the bank, run its rapids, pursue its course to "get" the whole river. Instead, I come away with only snapshots.

So, how do we get to know and understand what our lives are really about and where we're really going? I'd suggest that the answers come *from the results*. Everything explained above boils down to the fact that we humans are creatures of habit. If something happens once, it may be an accident; if it happens twice, be suspicious; if it happens three times, the odds are that you've got a pattern. And by grasping the meaning of that pattern, you can begin to tell something about the underlying direction of your life.

An example to put flesh on that conclusion: If I fall in love—

once—with someone who is emotionally unavailable, it may be an unlucky accident. But if that happens again and again, it makes sense to conclude that I have within me some unspoken but very powerful guidance system that leads me to people who are emotionally unavailable. It's what I'm "supposed" to do, just as water is "supposed" to flow to the sea. I can get angry at that pattern. I can deny it. I can refuse to look at it. But if it keeps happening, probably I've got living proof in myself of the old AA saying, "If it quacks like a duck, and swims like a duck, and waddles like a duck, and flies like a duck . . . most likely it's a duck."

What is it that keeps me homing in on people who are the exact opposite of what I really need in my life? What is this inner "radar" that constantly and consistently leads me to death and destruction instead of fulfillment and life? What kept me convinced with granitelike stubbornness that I needed my drugs and alcohol to live, even as they were killing me? What keeps client after client believing that the whippings and abusive batterings they got from their alcoholic/dysfunctional parents were "character building" and "good for them" and that their childhoods were not "that bad"? What is this belief that keeps us looking through the wrong end of the telescope, that so bewitches us that we see chemical dependency's Wonderland as more enticing than life itself?

All these questions have a one-word answer: *denial.*

You see, habitual denial is not just a symptom—or even *"the* identifying and presenting symptom"—of alcoholism and addiction. Rather, it's the very bedrock, the foundation, the channeled riverbed of belief without which chemical dependency cannot exist.

And So . . .
A Definition of Chemical Dependency

In my opinion, the most important insight AA has brought to recovery for alcoholics and addicts is the first step of its Twelve-Step program: "We admitted that we were powerless over alcohol—that our lives had become unmanageable." In the lives of AA members, this step has translated again and again into a paradoxical phenomenon: At that point in time when practicing alcoholics can admit and accept that they are alcoholics, accept that they *do* have a problem with alcohol, they can stop being victimized by their drinking. They can quit.

And the opposite is true. If alcoholics cannot come to such an acceptance, no matter what treatment they undergo or how much willpower they exert, they will very probably drink again. Or, if they do not drink, they will soon start to practice another form of compulsive behavior, such as "workaholism," sexual addiction, or religious fanaticism. In the long run, these are addictions in their own right, and as deadly as compulsive drinking and drugging.

In short, it is only when alcoholics break through their denial that they have a hope for genuine recovery. The denial has to be shattered first; then the compulsive behavior can cease.

This brings us to my own definition of chemical dependency: "It is a disease of physiological addiction to alcohol (or drugs) necessarily founded upon a progressive belief system of denial that results in destructive compulsive behavior." More simply, *without a belief system of denial, you can't have alcoholism!*[1]

---

[1] To illustrate, many people become physiologically addicted to painkilling drugs after operations or when dealing with chronic severe hurts and maladies. Nevertheless, by far the greater majority of them, when the time comes to quit their medication, do so. They pass through a period of discomfort (sometimes even severe discomfort) withdrawing from their drugs, and then they get on with their lives. They can do so simply because they knew what they were doing from the beginning; they chose to do what they had to do to deal with their particular problems; and, most important, they were not in denial about the effects of the drugs.

Chapter 2

If Your Lips Are Moving, You're Lying

Chemically Dependent People and Their Denial
The Disease and Deadliness of Dependency

An AA sponsor is a "Big Brother," best friend, and guide in sobriety rolled into one. Mine is an eccentric, brilliant, curmudgeonly good old boy named Alva. I met him at the first AA meeting I attended. He's a lawyer who once defended a raccoon named Rocky against the state of Washington—and won. Usually, however, he chooses to work only with chemical abusers and their families.

To deal with people "not according to their wants but according to their needs," as he says, Alva has a unique lie detector in his office: an eight-by-ten-inch, empty picture frame with a handle attached to one side. Clients come in; Alva asks them to tell their stories, then stares at them through the picture frame as they speak. Eventually, their curiosity wins out, and they ask what he's doing. He replies that the picture frame is his personal polygraph machine. He studies them through it and then informs them, "If your lips are moving, you're lying."

At that point, clients can only get angry or laugh. To which Alva says, "Now you're telling the truth! The only part of you that can't lie is your feelings."

Understandably, some clients don't last beyond a first session, but those who do—based on results—have a good chance of getting sober and rebuilding their lives.

In a nutshell, that picture of Alva putting clients through his personal polygraph test sums up for me both the meaning of alcoholism and the meaning of recovery.

The point of Alva's polygraph is that it forces his clients to realize that their words, their descriptions, their comprehensions, their understandings, their minds and intellects, do not and cannot tell their stories. Only their feelings can do that because, as a friend once said, their heads are ". . . broken."

In this chapter, I intend to use my own picture-frame polygraph, as it were, to turn things inside out and upside down, too—my reason for doing so is the same as Alva's. In chemical addiction, what we see is not what we get—what we think and comprehend and intellectually figure out about chemical dependency, what we can touch and feel and analyze, are but the symptoms, not the disease itself. For chemicals are not the villain, alcohol is not the point of alcoholism. Skid Road is not about weakness but strength; rather, its residents are the tough and hearty 10 percent or so who survived the disease long enough to come home. Conversely, the nonsensical fact is that drunks who "surrender" to being drunks suddenly no longer have to drink.

None of what I've just said makes any sense if you focus on the drugs, or the vomit of drunks, or the blank eyes of a heroin mainliner, or the horrors of a speed freak in withdrawal. But it can come clear if we concentrate on the abuser's belief system of denial. To get to an overview of that belief system of denial, let's peel off "a few layers of the onion." Let's look at the abuser's behavior, the lived experience of the chemically dependent person. We'll look through two sets of lenses: from within, with the abuser's own eyes; and from without, with the eyes of a detached observer. Then we'll face the question, "Why do alcoholics and addicts behave the way they do?" The answer will bring us face-to-face with denial as a belief system. It will make us focus not on the symptomatic behavior—the drugs taken, the alcohol drunk, the abusive behavior acted out—but on the underlying condition that causes and allows that behavior to happen.

Starting at the Bottom

I was very sick and chemically toxic during my first two years of sobriety, and consequently have few distinct memories of that time. But I will never forget the experience of my first AA meeting. Nobody else there had been what I'd been or lived as I had lived; none of them could "tell my story" as his or her own. I didn't particularly like those people, yet I could identify with each of them. In spite of myself, I'd come home . . . dammit!

I had just spent the previous days on "the bottom." I wish I had some examples, some stories about this time, to share with you as an illustration of what the bottom experience is like . . . but I don't. For me, it was not a time of catastrophic tragedy or explosive devastation. It was not even a time of drunkenness. It was just three days of sitting in a chair at my sister's house, utterly quiet, utterly isolated, utterly empty—knowing only one fact, somehow staring it in the face: that I was a drunk, and nothing, *nothing,* more. I can't explain how it came to be; I just woke up one morning and knew that truth. My truth.

The bottom is absolutely the most isolated, alone place a human being can ever be. For me, the greatest pain of it was that I knew, I *knew,* I was totally disconnected; and more, that there was no hope of ever reconnecting again. One of my favorite writers, G. K. Chesterton, writes, "It is one of the million wild jests of truth that we can know nothing until we know nothing."[1] "Bottom," for me, was the "place" where I knew that I knew nothing. Worse, I really didn't care.

But here, in the dank basement of a dilapidated Methodist church, sat a group of people who had seen the same "nothing" and with whom I belonged—not in spite of who I was, but because of it. I was the same as they, and it was all very confusing. I resisted them, and I still often resist today, but over all the intervening time, *that I belonged* is the one truth I've never been able to successfully shake.

[1] Gilbert Keith Chesterton, *Heretics* (New York: John Lane, 1905), p. 65.

A Little History

In the past fifty years or so, many people have earned their Ph.D.'s studying chemical abuse. Even more notable, chemicals—especially alcohol—and their effects on the human system support the jobs and careers of thousands of counselors, cops, treatment-center staff, and government bureaucrats, not to mention smugglers, pushers, distillers, brewers, and advertising personnel. Today, chemicals are the stuff not only of academic respectability but of big business and big government.

Thus, commenting about the drug scene demands a certain delicacy; you never know whose financial or professional ox you're going to gore. Let me take a couple of pages here for an extended example. For many years, many people in the field of treatment have invested great amounts of thought, emotion, time, and courage developing an understanding of alcoholism or addiction as an illness, a disease. In my opinion, their work compels attention and respect for many reasons, the most important being the results they've generated for people they help to heal. The recovery rate for addicts and alcoholics is dismal, but (I suspect) for the first time in history there is a genuine, growing hope for more than just the occasional, exceptional success.

The insight that leads observers to conclude that chemical dependency is a disease is a simple, inescapable fact—as the psychiatrist at the treatment center I attended used to say, "Alcoholic people behave in alcoholic ways." That is, despite the uniqueness of each individual abuser, *the plot is always the same.* Each of us goes about doing our alcoholic things in our individual way, but we all play out the same dreary theme. God forbid, but we're predictable!

George Jellinck, one of the pioneers in developing the "disease concept of alcoholism," graphed it all out on a chart that's as valid today as it was in the forties. Later researchers have modified it to describe not only alcoholism but other chemical addictions as well.

No matter what our social background—or wealth, or profession, or ethnic heritage, or religion, or you name it—our dependency is always, almost boringly, the same. We drank our drinks and did our drugs; and as we did, we acted out the behavior, progressed through the stages of the disease, and ended up tapping death on the shoulder.

Again, my experience is mine uniquely, but the pattern is universal for all alcoholics in recovery . . . including the resistance. Thus, I'm convinced we're back to the saying that what seems to be a duck is most likely a duck. Like schizophrenia or diabetes, chemical addiction has specific symptoms, specific behaviors, a specific progression, and (if left untreated) a specific conclusion . . . death. *It makes sense* to call chemical dependency a "disease."

But—and this is where I may gore an ox or two—just to show that chemical dependency is a disease *is not enough*. It is more—and that "more" needs to be spelled out and spoken honestly.

Ordinary Behavior

Alcoholic people behave in alcoholic ways, and alcoholic ways are to batter, lie, cheat, philander, despair, and then to die. To cut to the heart of the matter: Alcoholic behaviors are evil and immoral.

I say this in sorrow, not judgment or guilt. I am not a Fundamentalist tub-thumping against "Demon Rum." *Evil* and *immoral* are ugly words. I don't like them. I don't like the risk I take in using them. Yet I am convinced that if we do not use *these words* to describe the full truth about our "disease," we remain in denial, unable to heal.

So, let me define what I mean when I use these two words. By *evil* I mean what the thinkers of the Middle Ages meant: the absence of what should be there, an absence of the good. For example, human relations should be marked by understanding, justice, and acceptance. So, when prejudice, oppression, and distrust hold sway, the times are evil—they are not as they should be.

Likewise, by *immoral* I mean what happens to men and women when they live in ways that dehumanize themselves or others. An example: The perpetrators of the Holocaust in Nazi Germany, because they ripped life from most of their victims and made the remainder the "walking dead," were immoral. One could not sur-

THE PROGRESSIVE DISEASE OF ALCOHOLISM

(READ FROM LEFT... DOWN, RIGHT... UP!)

ADDICTION

RECOVERY

HEAVY SOCIAL DRINKING · 5 OR MORE PER OCCASION · 2 OR MORE TIMES WEEKLY

ENLIGHTENED AND INTERESTING WAY OF LIFE OPENS UP WITH ROAD AHEAD TO HIGHER LEVELS THAN EVER THOUGHT POSSIBLE

2 YEARS (AVERAGE)

2 TO 25 YEARS

- INCREASE IN ALCOHOL TOLERANCE
- DESIRE TO CONTINUE WHEN OTHERS STOP
- DRINKING TO RELIEVE TENSION
- DRINKING BEFORE A DRINKING FUNCTION
- UNCOMFORTABLE IN SITUATION WHERE THERE IS NO ALCOHOL
- RELIEF DRINKING COMMENCES
- PREOCCUPATION WITH ALCOHOL (THINKING ABOUT NEXT DRINK)
- OCCASIONAL MEMORY LAPSES AFTER HEAVY DRINKING
- SECRET IRRITATION WHEN YOUR DRINKING IS DISCUSSED

THE 9 SIGNS OF ALCOHOLISM

HELP NEEDED

- RETURN OF RESPECT OF FAMILY AND FRIENDS
- IMPROVED PEACE OF MIND
- CONFIDENCE OF EMPLOYER BEGINS
- RATIONALIZATION RECOGNIZED
- FIRST STEPS TOWARDS ECONOMIC STABILITY
- INCREASE OF EMOTIONAL CONTROL
- ADJUSTMENT TO FAMILY NEEDS
- CONTINUOUS COMFORTABLE FEELING OF SOBRIETY BEGINS
- FULL APPRECIATION OF SPIRITUAL VALUES
- BEGIN CONTENTMENT IN SOBRIETY
- INCREASED INTEREST/ACTIVITY IN GROUP THERAPY
- NEW INTERESTS DEVELOP
- NEW FUTURE FACED WITH DETERMINATION AND COURAGE
- DESIRE TO ESCAPE PASSES

LOSS OF CONTROL PHASE — RATIONALIZATION BEGINS

- LYING ABOUT DRINKING TO EVERYBODY (RATIONALIZATION)
- INCREASING FREQUENCY OF RELIEF DRINKING
- URGENCY OF FIRST DRINK
- SNEAKING DRINKS
- INCREASING DEPENDENCE ON ALCOHOL
- DRINKING BOLSTERED WITH EXCUSES
- FEELING OF GUILT ABOUT DRINKING
- INCREASED MEMORY BLACKOUTS
- UNABLE TO DISCUSS PROBLEMS
- TREMORS AND EARLY MORNING DRINKS
- PROMISES AND RESOLUTIONS FAIL REPEATEDLY
- COMPLETE DISHONESTY
- LOSS OF OTHER INTERESTS
- GRANDIOSE AND AGGRESSIVE BEHAVIOR
- EFFORTS TO CONTROL FAIL REPEATEDLY
- FAMILY, WORK AND MONEY PROBLEMS
- FAMILY AND FRIENDS AVOIDED
- NEGLECT OF FOOD
- DRINKING ALONE — SECRETLY

- NEW SET OF MORAL VALUES STARTS UNFOLDING
- NEW CIRCLE OF STABLE FRIENDS
- SOME SELF ESTEEM RETURNS
- NATURAL REST AND SLEEP
- DIMINISHING FEARS AND ANXIETIES
- FAMILY AND FRIENDS APPRECIATE EFFORTS
- BEGINNING OF REALISTIC THINKING
- APPLICATION OF SPIRITUAL VALUES BEGINS
- REGULAR NOURISHMENT TAKEN
- DESIRE FOR GROUP THERAPY GROWS
- SPIRITUAL NEEDS EXAMINED

RADICAL DETERIORATION OF FAMILY RELATIONSHIPS

NOW THINKS: "ACTIVITIES INTERFERE WITH MY DRINKING..."

LOSS OF JOB

- PHYSICAL DETERIORATION
- MORAL DETERIORATION
- URGENT NEED FOR MORNING DRINK
- UNREASONABLE RESENTMENTS
- "WATER WAGON" ATTEMPTS FAIL
- LOSS OF WILL POWER
- ONSET OF LENGTHY DRUNKS
- GEOGRAPHICAL ESCAPE ATTEMPTED
- IMPAIRED THINKING
- DRINKING WITH INFERIORS
- SUCCESSIVE LENGTHY DRUNKS
- INDEFINABLE FEARS
- UNABLE TO WORK
- OBSESSION WITH DRINKING
- SANITARIUM OR HOSPITAL
- PERSISTENT REMORSE
- LOSS OF FAMILY
- DECREASE IN ALCOHOLIC TOLERANCE
- HOSPITAL/SANITARIUM
- UNABLE TO INITIATE ACTION
- ALL ALIBIS EXHAUSTED

- DAWN OF NEW HOPE
- ATTEMPTS AT HONEST THINKING
- DESIRE FOR ALCOHOL PERSISTS
- CARE OF PERSONAL APPEARANCE/HYGIENE BEGINS
- STARTS TO REACT TO GROUP THERAPY
- ATTEMPTS TO STOP DRINKING
- LEARNS ALCOHOLISM A DISEASE
- MEETS RECOVERED, NORMAL, HAPPY ALCOHOLICS
- DRYING OUT/MEDICAL HELP?

DERELICTION
DRINKING AWAY "SYMPTOMS OF DRINKING" IN VICIOUS CIRCLES

COMPLETE ABANDONMENT

COMPLETE DEFEAT ADMITTED · CALLS FOR HELP

CONTINUED DETERIORATION

DEATH

25 YEARS

1/2 TO 18 YRS AVERAGE

EARLY

MIDDLE

1 TO 6 YRS AVERAGE

2-10 YEARS

2 TO 10 YEARS

LATE

© Doyle F. Lindley, 1968

vive as recognizably human in the camps, either as a prisoner or as a guard.

The Holocaust was evil and immoral. The Killing Fields were evil and immoral. Slavery is evil and immoral—and addiction is slavery. There comes a point in our drinking and using when we cannot *not* drink and use. Some of us fight that bondage; some of us give in; but we all face it. Slavery is the root issue; evil and immorality are its truth.

When we abusers drank and used, in order to drink and use, we (usually and commonly) stole from, lied to, and cheated the people we loved the most. Love, justice, honesty, caring—those are not hallmarks of the practice of our disease. With the passage of time, most of us (especially those of us who survived long enough to make it to Skid Road or its suburbs) had less and less about ourselves that could be called human or humane. We had become empty.

I know many drinkers and users. I know them in the practice of their disease and in the practice of their recovery. Some are bright; some are boors; some I'd take home to Mother; some I wouldn't allow within a hundred paces of my sister or brother. Yet I don't know one of us who really wanted and decided to become a lying, cheating, fraudulent, philandering drunk. It's just not an attractive blueprint for life. Something happened: We got sucked in and trapped; we ended up empty and dehumanized; we became evil and immoral.

So we ask, "Why me? Other people drink; other people seem to use other drugs recreationally; they didn't end up like me. How come me and not them?" The answer has several parts to it.

Why Me?

The first part has to do with biology, physiology, and genetics. Since I'm no expert in those subjects, I have to draw on the thought and research of others.

The prevailing opinion today seems to be that there's no single cause of alcoholism/addiction in any given person. A good picture

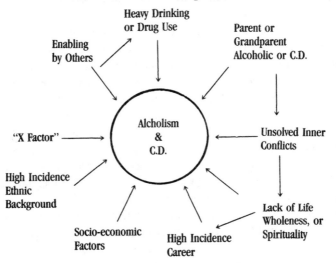

Mosaic Theory of the Etiology of Alcoholism and Other Chemical Dependence

Enabling by Others

Heavy Drinking or Drug Use

Parent or Grandparent Alcoholic or C.D.

"X Factor"

Alcholism & C.D.

Unsolved Inner Conflicts

High Incidence Ethnic Background

Socio-economic Factors

High Incidence Career

Lack of Life Wholeness, or Spirituality

Although the etiology of alcoholism in unknown, enough is known about it to postulate that it is probably multifactorial (Ewing & Rouse 1978; Whitfield 1983). Health workers view several other chronic illnesses in this way, with hypertension and diabetes mellitus being but two examples.

One can find at least eight categories of possible contributory factors or etiologies for alcoholism. Probably the most convincing is *parental history of problem drinking*. The children of alcoholics are at higher risk for developing alcoholism than are those in the general population (Goodwin 1971). If both of one's parents are alcoholic, the risk of becoming alcoholic probably exceeds 50 pecent. At times, the illness will skip one generation, usually when people choose to abstain from using alcohol or other drugs, often because *their* own parent was alcoholic. However, most children of alcoholics deny that their parent was so, although some may use terms like "My mother drank too much," or "My father had an occasional problem with drinking."

Perhaps an equally convincing cause is *heavy drinking or drug use*. At least 5% of heavy drinkers become alcoholic every year. One can estimate that from 25 to 75% of persons dependent upon other drugs, excluding caffeine and tobacco, either are or become alcoholic at some time during their lives.

Probably the third strongest causal factor is the phenomenon known as *enabling*. Enabling means reacting to symptoms of alcoholism in another person in such a way as to shield the alcoholic from experiencing the full impact of the harmful consequences of the disease. Gradually, those enablers who are close to the alcoholic develop a condition called co-alcoholism, described above (Whitfield 1984). A helping professional may become an enabler by not recognizing or making the diagnosis of either alcoholism or co-alcoholism, by treating the alcoholism solely as a symptom of "underlying psychopathol-

(cont'd)

ogy," or by not referring the person for an evaluation or for treatment. Because they received little training in professional school on alcoholism as a primary illness, and because it is now such a treatable condition, many helping professionals are seeking such skills through books and workshops that address this area.

The *"X Factor"* may be related to inheritance, and may even be acquired. It includes such *biological* phenomena that are common among alcoholics, such as loss of control, memory blackouts, a lack of hangovers early in alcoholism (Whitfield 1985), a more marked P and alpha brain wave response to alcohol, abnormal acetaldehyde metabolism, and less intoxication and body sway on drinking (Goodwin 1971 & 1982). Over half of alcoholics appear to manifest at least three of these involuntary phenomena.

Ethnic background and career are also factors. For example, second and third generation Irish Catholics and Scandinavian Americans have a higher prevalence of alcoholism than do Italians and Orientals. High incidence *careers* include, in roughly estimated decreasing prevalence: liquor industry workers and bartenders, entertainers, writers, military personnel, physicians and possibly

other health professionals. *Socio-eco-nomic* factors are also influential, as well as are *cultural* factors such as the *media,* which push alcohol and other substances upon the public many times each day. Also important is a *lack of meaning or spirituality* in the person's life . . .

Unsolved inner conflicts may be due to growing up in an alcoholic and co-alcoholic family, or may result from other causes, including life in general. Interestingly, "psychological problems" are often considered by the general public and by many mental health workers as being the most common *cause* of alcoholism. However, if one treats the patient from this approach alone, it is unlikely that a successful recovery will be achieved. These remarks are not to discount the importance of treating unsolved internal conflicts that usually develop *during* and *from* the person's addiction, and often from growing up in an alcoholic home.

Because alcoholics often suffer as a result of using other drugs, and vice versa, . . . we now view this condition as one illness, which we call *chemical dependence.* The principles of treatment are the same for each, whether it be alcoholism or another drug problem.

of the many contributing factors is presented on the following page, which I've borrowed from Dr. Charles L. Whitfield, M.D.[2]

What all of this indicates is that the more of those factors I've got lined up against me, the more the odds of my becoming chemically dependent jump astronomically. (In my case, it was almost a lead-pipe cinch. I'm the Irish-Scottish-German-Norwegian, Catholic grandson of an alcoholic. Mix me and alcohol, and you get the "ism"). I hate to acknowledge that kind of determinism, but ever since I started to go bald, I've had to surrender (most ungraciously) to the power of genes.

[2]Charles L. Whitfield, M.D., *Alcoholism, Attachments & Spirituality: A Transpersonal Approach* (East Rutherford, NJ: Thomas W. Perrin, 1985), p. 4.

The next part of the answer is harder to get to and not so mathematical.

The place to begin is a discussion of the conscious reasons we drank or used. I think an exact list of all those reasons would be as long as a list of the names of every person who ever bent an elbow, puffed a weed, stuck himself with a needle, or popped a pill. Yet, as numerous as those reasons are, I believe they can all be summed up with a single statement: We used our drug or drugs of choice *because they worked.* And how they worked was very simple: They changed our sense and perception of reality; they made us see ourselves and the people and the things around us differently. Some of us fat ones they made thin; short ones they made tall; tense ones they relaxed; withdrawn ones they made outgoing; sad ones they made happy; grieving, burned-out ones they made numb. (They almost made me believe I had hair.) They worked . . . and worked . . . and worked.

In our discovery that drugs and alcohol work, I doubt that we abusers are different from the rest of people. A neuropharmacologist friend of mine likes to point out that there are three legitimate uses for drugs and alcohol: as medicine, as part of religious ceremonies, and as catalysts for communal celebrations. In each of those uses, alcohol and drugs are employed because they work, because they alter perceptions and/or change feelings.

But to use chemicals in those "legitimate" situations, even large amounts of chemicals, is usually not addictive for the simple reason that these occasions are out of the ordinary. They are apart from the normal, daily rhythms of our lives. And this "extraordinariness," this "exceptionality" of the medicinal, religious, and celebrative use of drugs is maintained by two very strong controls. The first is the strict boundaries set by society, i.e., doctors, priests, and communities regulate the kinds and amounts of the drugs employed. The second, I believe, is the simple preference most people have to live their lives in contact with things as they are, undistorted by chemically altered perceptions. Most humans like the earth to stay stable as they walk it.

Here, alcoholics and addicts begin to depart from the majority of people. By preference, for whatever reasons, we choose *not* to face the world as it is. We like it better, we feel more comfortable in it, when our chemicals have done their job and made things as we want them to be—or at least smoothed down the rough edges of reality. Some of us do that almost daily, others only occasionally, but the result is the same—"better" living through chemical buffering. At least, it sure seems better at the time.

The times become more and more frequent, which brings us to perhaps the one final and overriding ingredient to alcoholism, the one final constituent in the answer to the question, "Why me?" *Habit.* I believe that habit is at one and the same time the least thought about and most important element of the disease.

Habits

The reason habits are both so little considered and so highly important is simply that they're so obvious, and we usually overlook the obvious. That's the whole point about habits anyway: They free us for the important things of life by removing our need to think about the ordinary, daily stuff we're doing. It's probably impossible to get an exact percentage, but no one can deny that an extremely high proportion of our daily life is lived under the guidance system of our habits.

In fact, it's no exaggeration to say that our habits are the means by which we establish personal ownership of our lives. For example: There are many ways to put on a pair of pants, but once I've established my habitual way of doing it—by standing, let's say, pulling on the right leg before the left—that style of "doing it" passes from being just one of several *possible* courses of action to *my* way of behaving. I own it; even more significantly, it owns me.

So, for us abusers, using chemicals to change our perception of reality becomes our normal, ordinary, habitual way of living. For us, there is nothing exceptional or extraordinary about it; it has become our personal style. What was once a way of behaving has evolved (for us) into *the* way to live. We've developed an entire lifestyle of denial, and so Alva's right: If our lips are moving, we're lying.

A pivotal point about the power of habits: The less time we've had them, the easier it is to shake them. About six years ago, I started swimming to get in condition and, up until several months ago, went to the pool faithfully three or four times a week. Then last Christmas, I got sick for about a month. Getting back into that routine has been more than slightly difficult ever since.

Putting on my pants is a different story. I started doing that about forty-three years ago. To test what I've been writing about, I recently tried pulling on my pants left leg first, instead of right, for a week. Every day I could remember to do it (which was the first challenge), that little exercise disoriented my morning, made me cranky, threw off my rhythms for a good part of the day, and actually caused me emotional pain. I found that when I disrupted that "insignificant" little habit, I was forced to start thinking and making decisions throughout the whole course of getting up and ready for the day ahead. And, if there's anything I find painful early in the morning, it's thinking and making decisions.

To sum up, then, the facts lead me to perceive three elements to alcoholism: an actual physiological dependence on chemicals, a preference for the altered view of reality chemicals induce, and the habit of actually using chemicals to bring about that altered state of experiencing things. That much seems clear.

But right when we get to this point of clarity, it's time to muddy the waters again. As I mentioned in the first chapter, the Big Book of AA calls alcoholism "cunning, baffling and powerful." And nowhere does the "baffling" nature of the disease manifest itself more obviously than when alcoholics and addicts quit drinking and using.

There's the physical process of withdrawal from the chemicals— one of the more painful, crazy-making experiences a human can undergo. (There have been times in the past nine years when the only thing that kept me from drinking again was to remember how much it hurt to get off the stuff the first time around.)

Of itself, getting rid of the chemicals does nothing but create a hole in the abuser's lifestyle. The absence of drugs did not substantially change my preference for an altered perception of reality— or my habit of reaching out for something to bring about that altered state. Members of AA, for example, often say that drinking is just a symptom of alcoholism, and not even a necessary one. (Suddenly, we're back to Clancy I. and his dying drunks protesting, "It wasn't the booze.")

Once again, the opposite of everything is true. The thing everyone can see and touch, and hate; the thing we've named the disease for; the thing against which we pass legislation and mount national crusades, namely "alcohol and drugs," is not even the main ingredient of the disease of alcoholism.

Altered States

Take away an addict's chemicals, and all you get is an addict without chemicals: frightened, mean, desperate, and angry. Spouses often find themselves telling a partner who's gone on the wagon, "I liked you better when you were drunk." The sad fact is that abusers who've done nothing but stop drinking still behave in habitually alcoholic ways—by this point, that's all they know how to do.

The conclusion is inevitable. The real guts of the disease is *the abuser's preferred and habitual practice of living in a state of altered consciousness*—his habit of living in denial. I know many people who have stopped drinking and using. Most of them didn't stay stopped for long, but there are some who, by determination and willpower, actually have stayed dry and clean. Of the latter, however, I know of none who have been able to break out of their lifestyle of denial simply and only by stopping their chemical intake.

Let's return to Jellinck's chart to explain. It lists forty-three symptoms in the progression of chemical dependency, but only fourteen have to do with the actual actions of drinking or using. The remaining twenty-nine name attitudinal and behavioral changes in the progression of the disease. So, as well as describing a disease pattern of chemical intake, Jellinck's chart outlines the development of an entire lifestyle, a chemically abusive way of living. Anyone in recovery can tell you that it's a lifestyle defined by grandiosity, aggressiveness, dishonesty, stealth, half-truth, compulsive rationalization, avoidance, self-pity, and growing isolation—among other attractive traits.

If you look at all these attitudes and behaviors as an exercise in the abuser's preference for changing his view of reality, it quickly becomes clear that the actual act of drinking is only part of the overall problem.

When you consider that this preferred lifestyle of denial has become even more habitual to an abuser than his chemical intake, you can begin to appreciate why this disease is so damnably hard to confront. If the booze doesn't get you, the denial will. Most alcoholics and addicts do die before their time—and for no other reason than that . . . they are alcoholics and addicts.

For the drinker, what was once a possible lifestyle has become his lifestyle; what was once a way of living has become the way of doing it. I cannot emphasize this too strongly because it is here, at the point where a possible way of living became my personal, habitual defined way of living, that I laid the foundation for my alcoholic belief system.

The progression is not necessarily logical, but it is very human: from *a* way to *my* way, to *the* way, to the way it *should* be. And, as soon as we start dealing with "shoulds," we're dealing with beliefs. It's no coincidence that the theologians of the Middle Ages defined faith—belief—as a "habit."

Any student of human nature will tell you we humans live not by our knowledge or our logic but by our beliefs. We just don't have the time or capacity to do otherwise. Such students also tell us that the most natural thing in the world is for individual persons to seek out and congregate with others who believe and live as they do. It's too uncomfortable and upsetting to do otherwise. Imagine what it would be like to live as the "different one," as the freak—constantly open to criticism and question.

Small wonder that alcoholics and addicts seek out alcoholics and addicts. As I recall, we all even had the same odor (although the discerning nose could distinguish the gin drinkers from the lovers of Scotch). We all shared common feelings and experiences. It may have been a kind of anticommunity characterized by denial and isolation, but no bartender worth his salt ever forgot my drink after the second round, no fellow drunk begrudged me one for the road. I belonged.

A Modest Comparison

Would it sound blasphemous to compare the regulars at the local pub to the congregation of the Calvary Temple down the street? Well, the fundamental elements are the same: a place to gather, a community of support, a ritual to observe, a system of belief, and even—for us High Church aficionados—a sacrament to consume.

I make this religious comparison to highlight the power of the alcoholic style of life. Look at Northern Ireland, Iran, the rise of the "religious right" in our own country. Protest all you want that it's unenlightened and foolish to be religious in today's world, but the power of religion, its hold, and its ability to regenerate itself cannot be denied. Whether or not you agree with him, try to name a hotter "political property" in the world today (with the exception of Gorbachev) than Pope John Paul II. Remember all those who have died with "God wills it!," or "There is no God but Allah!" on their lips.

Besides that of religion, the only belief system, the only lifestyle, in human history that has killed so many is the habitual denial we call alcoholism and addiction.

Chapter 3

The Most Dangerous Words

Codependent Belief and Denial

Man's Best Friend

I have one nearly perfect relationship (of course, no late-stage, co-dependent alcoholic would allow himself one that was significantly less than perfect). It's defined by strict rules of contract and possession. There are clear rituals for how we attend to each other, a kind of daily minuet choreographed by partners whose whole and sole aim is to please one another. We've become custodians of each other's needs.

Today, Loki is probably the one living being to whom I feel I can say, "I love you," without risk and with complete impunity. I can trust him never to betray my love, nor to abandon me. Loki is a two-year-old, ninety-five-pound Alsatian-Labrador (a German shepherd with floppy ears, liquid eyes, and humongous paws). He loves to goose me when I undress at night, and positively demands (and gets) far too many Milk Bones for his own good. Unlike many dogs, he's amazingly secure about his food: A visiting hound can safely eat from his dish anytime, but God help the dog who tries to steal off with his rawhide bone or squeaky toy. The clear order of his priorities is play, love, and food. He's my first dog. I almost lost him when he was seven months old to an intestinal infection; my heart felt as if it would break.

I'm a forty-six-year-old, six-foot, 190-pound, balding redhead—very good at being serious, big, and professionally helpful. I don't find it easy to unbend, to socialize for the sake of socializing, or to relax into spontaneous playfulness. I know the inside of human pain intimately, and am usually superb in crisis; I am fierce in my protectiveness of those for whom I care. But when it comes to small talk, banter, and routine (the "ordinary" that constitutes most of life), I'm most likely to be awkward and boring.

So Loki and I fit hand in glove. He gets me to play and laugh daily. I feed him, care for his hurts, and give him security. He cajoles, whines, and demands me out of myself. I set minimal boundaries, spoil him, and provide him the sanctuary he needs to stay puppylike. It's an altogether pleasing partnership that crests with tender intensity when we go driving at night and he sprawls asleep across the front seat of the car with his head in my lap.

I grant you, pets can be romanticized to the point of absurdity, and any relationship can be analyzed to death. Yet what happens between Loki and me, or any animal and its human, can be used as a metaphor about the connections between chemical abusers and their "significant others."

There's a saying around Twelve-Step meetings that we abusers and our partners don't form relationships—we take hostages. Like most program sayings, that bit of painfully refined wisdom hits the bull's-eye.

Loki's and my relationship is as it is supposed to be, for dogs are supposed to be taken hostage by their humans. Loki is supposed to be codependent: He is supposed to have only the control—i.e., the ability to manipulate me into doing what he wants and needs. I am supposed to have the power, the ability to say yes or no. When he whines at the door, I probably *will* choose to let him out; when he plays hangdog, I probably *will* feel guilty—but I may not. Wherever I go, he's no more than three feet behind. *He cannot do otherwise.* I could choose to abandon him, but he could not choose to leave me. There's a paradox here: For all of his ability to get me to do what he wants, Loki has to live in complete trust that I will continue to choose to do as I have done and care for him. But despite my feelings for him and the guilt I might feel, I really am free to stop caring, to leave him. I don't have to trust, because I know he can't leave me. In short, I am his "Higher Power."

It's a bit different in adult human relations. The possibility of mutual freedom, and therefore mutual risk, the need for mutual trust, makes human interconnecting a more complex experience. That freedom is the hub around which the craziness inherent to relationships between chemical abusers and their loved ones swirls.

The Mystery Word

No more than anyone else can I define love. But I know that if love is to be more than just hormonal urges and infatuations, it must involve acceptances, vulnerabilities, commitments, and choices that lead me ultimately to seek the good of my beloved. Nothing less will last. When my love begins, I may not be able to make that complete a gift of myself, but I have to be willing to grow to the point where I can. Nothing less than such a depth of willingness will survive the long haul.

Willingness, however, is not enough. I've also got to be *able* to do what I'm willing to do or else I live in self-deluding fantasy. Only with *both* willingness *and* ability can there be a hope of lasting, true love.

In twenty-some years as a priest and therapist, I've been privileged to have the crow's-nest view of a counselor on more relationships and marriages than I care to count. A lot of them have lasted; probably an equal number haven't. Of those that do last, some have done so because of pathology, laziness, or an inability on the part of one or both partners to see any way out of what seems to be an emotional dead end. But then there are the relationships that last and grow and deepen in mutual en*joy*ment; ongoing, accepting, nurturing love is their secret.

Fred, a local Al-Anon-AA village wit and friend, recently reminded me of a wonderful description of how codependents do relationships: "*We're* drowning, and it's *their* lives that flash before our eyes." Alva says it a little differently: "*They* drink and *we* hurt—and that's crazy." Any way you describe it, that kind of relating can only be called insane. Because, you see, there's a simple fact of human existence: We can only do for somebody else what we're already doing for ourselves. Christ knew that; Buddha knew that; and, God knows, Freud knew that (it's the insight behind his reflections on "projection").

So, in the case of those drowning codependents, if it's their lives flashing before our eyes as we go down for the third time, what we're actually seeing is not so much our love for them as it is our lack of love for ourselves.

I cannot imagine a stupider, more self-destructive, more doomed thing to do than to get involved or stay involved emotionally with a chemical abuser. We abusers, by the very fact we are abusers, have subordinated everyone and everything to our chemicals; we are living in denial; we are slowly committing suicide. Fall in love with us, and you're guaranteed to play second fiddle to a drug; you'll never get our real truth (we can't give what we ain't got); and you'll be the recipient of our suicidal anger (than which no anger is greater). Some bargain!

Every abuser I've met has had, at some level, an inkling of what he was doing to himself, some minimal intuition of his suicidal lifestyle, some sense of the depth of his self-*dis*respect. "I may not know who I am, but I do sense who I'm not. So how could I possibly really respect and love somebody stupid enough to respect or love me?"

Yet people not only fall in love with us; they stay with us. Codependents stick to us like flies to a honey pot. They fetch us our booze (and sometimes even drink with us). They warm our beds, and cover up with our bosses, and wipe up our vomit; they tell the neighbors we're "sick," and take care of the kids; they insist that the obituary columns of the newspapers say we died of heart disease or pancreatic cancer instead of alcoholism. They're useful people to have around.

Unfortunately, they sometimes wear down from it all and get depressed or stressed out and even occasionally die. But if they do die, it seldom takes long for us to find a replacement.

Thank God for codependents; it would be hard (impossible?) to be chemically dependent without them.

At this point in the first draft of this chapter, I apologized for being sarcastic. But as I thought about it, I realized there was no other way to drive home the sick craziness of the codependent reality: *They just won't stop coming back for more!* In fact, codependents keep coming back to us in exactly the same way we keep coming back to our substances. They're as addicted to us as we are to our drugs of choice.

Loki doesn't have a choice about making me his "Higher Power." His genes and generations of evolution have seen to that. He is not free, and that's the point. He truly has no options. The most he can have is control: if the "trust" he puts in me (which he cannot help but put in me) is well placed, he may be able to get me to do and be for him what he wants and needs me to do and be. That's the most he can "hope" for. And I've always got the power, the "ability to act" as *Webster's Ninth New Collegiate* calls it (or, as I said earlier, the "freedom"), because I can always choose to say no.

Codependent humans look much like Loki, especially if their relationships have been going on long enough to reach full bloom. Based on results, codependent after codependent gets to that point where he or she cannot leave, cannot *not* codepend. They have many excuses: "I stay for the sake of the kids"; "I promised for better or for worse"; "I'm too old to start over"; "I don't have what it takes to make it on my own." The truth is, in their guts they just can't leave. Or, if they do leave one abuser and then stay single for a long time, they'll still end up in a relationship with another one— and the dance just starts up all over again. It sounds like a drunk trying to stop drinking. . . .

The Great Charade

So far, then, codependency resembles Loki's relationship with me. But there is a difference that makes all the difference. Codependents are people, not dogs. People *can* leave. In contrast to Loki, their genes and their evolution are all about giving them precisely that choice. Nevertheless, codependents relate to their abusers as

Loki relates to me. That's the tragedy. At one and the same time, there are two completely contradictory realities going on inside co-dependents: They are physically free to leave, and that's a fact; yet they cannot leave because they are powerless over their addiction to us, and that's also a fact. What's more, practically every codependent I've known has at some level realized both of those facts, and has realized that they are both true. That, above all else, is the co-dependent agony. The opposite of everything is true.

There's a "con" going on somewhere—a very potent con, but a con nevertheless. Almost all the codependents I've known tell me that, as they try to break their emotional enslavement to their abusers, the thought of not having their beloved makes them feel as if they're "going to die." The real truth, however, is that they very well may die if they *stay with* their "beloved" abusers. Again, the opposite is true, and we're back to that *D*-word once more: *The core of the codependent's problem is a system of denial as potent and deep as that of the chemical abuser, and over which the codependent is equally as powerless.*

At this point, it's time to inspect the various parts of the codependent belief system of denial. But first let me own my own truth by affirming that I'm every bit as much a codependent as I am an alcoholic-addict. So far in this chapter, I've used the "third person" to talk about codependents. That was a helpful kind of verbal distancing for the analysis I wanted to present. From here on out, though, it's important that I claim my own codependent truth.

When I was in treatment in 1980, the viciousness of my mood swings and the sullen depth of my anger had my counselors convinced I'd been using other chemicals in addition to alcohol. I had the classic withdrawal symptoms of a dually addicted abuser. The normal stay at Guest House was ninety days; they kept me four-and-a-half months. It took that long to break through and reach some stability.

The honest-to-God truth was that I hadn't used any drugs but alcohol for over five years. So, in theory, my withdrawal just shouldn't have been so wicked and prolonged. Neither the staff nor I could figure out what was going on (I found out later that some of the counselors were not at all convinced I'd come clean with them about my drugging history). But, eventually, they did release me. About nine months later, after many AA and Al-Anon meetings, I finally figured out what I'd been going through: while in treatment withdrawing from alcohol, I'd also been breaking free from a personal relationship in which I'd been nothing if not classically, obsessively codependent. Since Guest House is a treatment center for Catholic priests—and since Catholic priests are not known for having "significant" personal relationships—it's not surprising that the staff wasn't able to put it all together. Even with the perspective of years, I can't say which part of that experience, the chemical withdrawal or the emotional one, was more painful. But I do know I never want to hurt like that again.

I *was* dually addicted; it was just that one of my addictions wasn't chemical[1] but, O Lordy, was it ever real! And so, from the ins and outs of my own journey, as well as from the lives of other codependents, I offer some reflections about codependency.

Still Crazy After All These Years

First, there's the blatant craziness of getting involved with a chemical abuser in the first place. A comparison to illustrate the point: Here in Washington State, just before Mount St. Helens blew its stack in 1980, an old, cantankerous character named Harry Truman gained some notoriety. He owned a lodge on Spirit Lake, at the base of the mountain, and refused to evacuate from his home as the eruption drew near. He claimed that Mount St. Helens was his friend and would never hurt him. Well, it blew, and he and his lodge got buried. They made a movie about old Harry, starring Art Carney, to romanticize his story; but the real, unvarnished truth is that Harry was a suicidal old fool. His blind denial got its logical, inevitable conclusion . . . death.

---

[1] Perhaps this assertion is too exclusive. Many would claim there's a chemically addictive element to codependency, also. Codependent relationships demand that their participants pump tremendous amounts of adrenaline as they try to live out their lies through each other. Adrenaline "rushes" are probably as addictive as those generated by speed and cocaine.

Because of the progressive nature of chemical addiction, anyone—*anyone*—who gets involved with an abuser sits on top of a
volcano, waiting for the eruption. The choice to live in such precarious circumstances lacks self-respect. Few things in life, other than
death and taxes, are inexorably inevitable, but the progressive degeneration of the chemically addicted abuser is one of them. Yet
we codependents stumble across such persons not just once in a
while, we're drawn to them hypnotically, like flies to cow pies. That
may not of itself make us certifiably insane, but it would give one
the distinct impression that we're operating one or two bricks short
of a load.

There's more. One of the infallible signs that you've got an alcoholic on your hands is the phrase "I can handle my liquor." Anyone
with sense enough to recognize that water flows downhill knows
he can't handle booze; that's why nonalcoholics are so careful about
its use. Likewise, codependents, by choosing to stay with their abusers, are implying a kind of nonsense that infallibly points to their
denial. They are saying by deed, if not also by word, that they can
"handle" their drinkers or users. Yeah, and by willpower and love
I can make my bald pate sprout hair. . . .

Codependents believe they can control their abusers' disease by
the application of enough love, care, determination, intelligence,
persuasion, stubbornness, guilt trips, and prayer. So they empty the
alcohol down the drain, flush the drugs, get angry, argue, throw the
bums out (and take them back again), and then suffer and die—
often before their beloved addicts and alcoholics expire. It's an excellent blueprint for martyrdom, but in my opinion it misses the
point of living.

Unavoidably, we have to face the question, "Why? Why do codependents codepend?" I doubt that anyone could supply a totally
satisfying response to that question, but the framework of an answer suggests itself if we take an in-depth look at how we codependents live out the craziness of our relationships.

Generally speaking, self-respecting people do self-respecting things,
and self-*dis*respecting people do disrespectful things to themselves.
In the beginning, many codependents have no more knowledge
than their partners that they're getting involved with somebody who's

going to end up as a junkie or a drunk. It usually takes a long time for addiction to develop, and many times the early signs of chemical dependency are the exact opposite from what you'd imagine. For example, I used to be the one who drove the drunk ones home because I could drink more and be less affected by it than anyone else. Only in treatment did I learn that hollow legs are one of the surest early signs of alcoholism. I thought it meant I could handle my booze, and my friends thought so, too. Some, indeed, thought it meant I didn't drink much at all. So, because of the sneaky nature of chemical dependency and the slow progression of the disease, in the beginning it's easy to get fooled.

But once the "beginning" has passed and the abuse has become obvious, why do codependents stick around? It's for the same reasons the abuser continues to abuse. In partnership and in parallel with our abusers, we build habit patterns of denial that eventually own us completely. *We end up codepending simply because we're codependents.*

The Empty Way to Love

Let's trace the progression. It starts with love and the normal things we humans do when we find ourselves in love. It's normal and good to be pleasing to those we love. It's normal and good to be accepting of those we love, to see the best in them and cherish it. It's normal and good for us not to expect or want our beloved to end up as a drunk or an addict. In the beginning, it's not normal to expect the worst.

Thus, we do the normal, good, and loving things that need to be done early in a relationship. We go through shakedown, adjust to individual quirks and differences, compromise when it's called for, and gradually get used to and comfortable with each other. We let go of the patterns and habits of our past lifestyles and set the foundation of a new life together. If we can (and so choose), we may beget children; we buy homes and establish careers. We compose a rhythm of living that develops through the normal stages: from *a* way, to *our* way, to *the* way, to the way it *should* be. We get grooved in. After all, isn't that what it means to love and live together?

But it's that very process of loving, accommodating, pleasing, accepting, and getting in the groove of life together that sets the foundation of codependency. For even as our life together gets constructed, something else is happening within our addicted loved ones; their disease is developing—not only their drinking and using but, more important, the patterns and habits of denial that undergird their chemical intake. And we, their codependents, in adjusting to and loving and pleasing persons whose sense of themselves is based more and more on denial—rather than reality—adjust, accommodate, love, please, and become conformed to their denial. We resonate with those we love. In other words, the only way we can live with someone who is in developing denial is to develop in denial ourselves.

Growing into a sense of one's self based on unreality is self-abusive. The conclusion follows quite logically. By the time our abusers' abuse becomes evident, more often than not we codependents have developed our own habit patterns of self-destructive denial. Consequently, like our abusers, we literally can't choose healthy options. The habits are too deep. Like the alcoholic and the addict, we're trapped. We, too, cannot *not* be in denial.

I believe codependent denial is far more subtle and harder to get to than that of the chemical abuser. There's nothing as concrete as a chemical substance on which to hang it. Our denial doesn't flow from some action as obviously unhealthy as drunkenness. It springs from our simple and good wish to love another human being well and fully.

I also suggest that the codependent style of loving receives a powerful boost from societal support and encouragement. Read something as classic as *Romeo and Juliet* or listen to your local country-and-western station; the message about the meaning of love is the same. One way or another the plays, the books, the songs, and the soaps all say our individual lives are empty and worthless unless we are united to some beloved "other." Life isn't worth living unless we're "in relationship."

Add that kind of societally imbued value system to the thoughts and feelings of somebody caught in the patterns of codependency, and you're guaranteed devastation, just as surely as flame plus gasoline fumes equal an explosion.

Codependent Denial

The cornerstone of codependency, then, is exactly the same as that of chemical dependency: an ever-deepening, habitual system of denial. Much like what abusers experience when their chemicals are removed, we codependents believe that, without our beloved ones, we're going to die. There's a predictable period and process of withdrawal after our relationships disintegrate. When drinkers and druggers cross over that "invisible line" and become chemically dependent, there's no turning back; they will remain dependent for the rest of their lives. So, too, for us codependents; once we got it, it "ain't gonna go away." The odds are statistically overwhelming: If we fall in love with an abuser once, we'll do it again and again.

There's another way we resemble our chemical abusers. We, too, prefer to live in an altered perception of reality. The only difference is how we change the way we see our world—not with chemicals but by the possession and use of the ones we love. When I'm in love, I can walk on water. When I have no "other one" to give my life validation and meaning, walking out the front door can be emotionally impossible.

In becoming codependent, I've passed an unconscious judgment on myself, and developed a basic belief. When I live in codependent denial, I am saying that fantasy and falsehood are of more value to me, are more important to me, than truth and reality. I am saying that my life has no meaning, no worth, without my fantasy, my denial, my beloved. But who in his right mind likes to spend time with somebody who believes himself worthless? Who wants to take on the job of being my reason for living? There are less taxing ways to spend an evening. But take away my beloved, and that's exactly what "codependent I" have to do: spend time with me, someone whose life I find empty and meaningless. How futile, and boring, and frightening! That's like asking me to keep company with a black hole. I'd rather find another drunk to love.

Lovers and Other Strangers

If you're the spouse, or lover, or close friend of a chemical abuser, and you find yourself saddened by, frightened by, angry about, or resistant to what I've said so far in this chapter, thank you. I've struck emotional pay dirt. I've employed these loaded words and painful pictures to insist that codependency is just as hurting, insane, progressive, and terminal a disease as chemical dependency.

But I'm not quite through. There's one last quirk that fixes the "Alice-in-Wonderland" quality of codependency (and causes the greatest bewilderment to anyone trying to understand what it's all about).

In the last chapter, we saw that the biggest paradox of alcoholism and addiction is that they are not "about" alcohol or drugs. In like fashion, codependency is not "about" the persons upon whom we are codependent. If you question codependents who've begun to face up to what's really been going on in their lives, one thing suddenly becomes clear: The names and faces may change, but *the obsessions, the feelings, the enabling and controlling behaviors, the pain, the stress, the craziness, the codependency, are always the same.* It doesn't matter with whom we fall in love; if we fall in love, our codependent tapes will start to run and we're off to the races—but it's always the *same* race, riding the *same* horse down the *same* track. Codependent people live and behave in codependent ways.

Approach things from the opposite direction, and the conclusion is the same. If you take away a junkie's drugs, all you get is a junkie without his fix: mean, desperate, scared, caught in denial. Likewise, take away the object of a codependent's affection, and all you get is a lonely codependent: controlling, scared, caught in the desperate denial belief that life will only have meaning when once again there is a beloved with whom one can relate. The loved one's gone, but the codependent remains—a codependent, nothing more, nothing less.

I've had three codependent love affairs in my life (so far). I played out all the themes we've discussed in this chapter with high drama and tragedy. In each of them, I began to self-destruct as soon as I spoke those three most dangerous words, "I love you." For each time I spoke these words, I literally felt a kind of "obligation" lock into place inside of me—an obligation to think, and feel, and believe, and understand, and react, and live as my loved one did. Suddenly, I felt obliged to be totally and only what my beloved wanted me to be. When I said, "I love you," I didn't *sell* the farm, I gave it away. And the second and third times around hurt even more than the first, because each time I had a horrible sense of *déjà vu*. I'd been there before, and here I was again. You see, it doesn't matter whom I fall for, *I do the same things*. My lovers are not the issue, I and my codependency are.

So, now, to turn the order of nature on its head, let me come back to Loki. Today, he serves for me as a gently wet-tongued metaphor of what a loving "Higher Power" should be like. (You may recall that I previously identified myself as *Loki's* higher power. As always, the opposite of everything *is* true.)

Loki recently cut his paw on a piece of glass. Three stitches and two antibiotic shots later, my bank account was lighter by $176.75. For myself, I'd think at least twice before shelling out $176.75 for three stitches; for him, I didn't even blink. Even at those prices, he's a wonderful bargain. Lopsided and unfree though our relationship may be, Loki, in his divinely doggy way, is teaching me a lesson that may change my life—if and when it sinks in. . . .

You see, I trust animals' intuition. I've never seen it fail. Loki sulks (I'm told) when he's not with me; I know he dances in delight when I return. He trusts me and loves me: If I'm holding him, he won't even snap at the vet who's sticking a needle in his haunch or sewing up his paw. Most of all, he believes in me. I'm not there yet; my codependency is still strong; but someday, if I can come to trust and love me as Loki does, I may reach a point where I can really, healthily love and trust another human being without losing myself.

Until then, though, I find myself more and more able to rest quietly (even when loneliness strikes), because I am learning that my life does have worth, richness, value, and fascination of itself.

Less and less do I have to depend on others for validation or meaning. I'm discovering the truth about me, the truth that Loki already knows.

At this point, the analogy of Loki breaks down. He is not human, he is not self-reflective. He may be codependent in his behavior, but Loki does not ask himself questions about his worth or worthiness as we do; he cannot. Those kinds of questions are both the blessing and the curse of being human.

Our codependency flows from those questions, from the beliefs we have about ourselves, while his flows simply from his genes and instincts. His "codependency," then, flows just from his being who and what he's supposed to be. Ours flows from our perception and belief that *we are not what we are supposed to be*—and it is that that makes all the difference.[2]

[2]For a list of codependent personality characteristics and behaviors, please consult Beattie, op. cit., pp. 37–45.

Chapter 4

It Really Was That Bad

Is Childhood Survivable?
Children of Alcoholics

They Thought It Was Just Another Class

I teach an eleven-week course on Adult Children of Alcoholics (ACOA). Ostensibly, the students who take the class do so as part of their training to become counselors and therapists, but what meets the eye is not all there is. There's a truism around Twelve-Step recovery meetings that nobody, absolutely nobody, comes to a meeting by accident. The same holds true for ACOA classes. Simply by counting raised hands, I've found out that over 90 percent of my students are adult children from alcoholic or otherwise dysfunctional families.

There are actually good, logical reasons for this, which will become clear as we continue. What's more important for me to point out here, however, is the kind of presumptions I can make as a teacher when I face these students. Every quarter, even though the faces and names change, it seems as if the people, the persons behind the faces, are the same.

And this is what I can presume: These are a group of tough survivors, master tacticians and practitioners of the arts of manipulation, avoidance, and strategic retreat. To a person, they will be far more adept at living in the world of the intellect, of their heads, than that of the gut and feelings. The majority of them will be "people pleasers" so attuned to me as an authority figure that they'll have learned to dance to any tune I might wish to play—long before I even realize I've a song in the offing. They will intuit any weakness or insecurity in me with uncanny accuracy. A few of them will be angry, raw, and ready to debate anything at the drop of a hat. A couple of others will be so skillful at camouflage and blending in that I'll never be able to learn their names. Some will be irresistibly cute, and others will have such an air of strength and security about them that my first intuitive response (I, who am no slouch at being a very big Big Daddy myself) will be to feel like a little boy again when I'm around them. Finally, I can presume that each one of those survivors, in his or her own way, will be convinced, no matter what kind of hell his childhood might have been, that it wasn't really all that bad. "After all, I only did what I needed to do to get through it, and I *did* survive . . . didn't I?"

The infallible sign that you've got a chemical abuser on your hands is the claim "I can handle my drugs." The equally infallible byword of ACOAs is "It really wasn't that bad." So, for the whole first half of the course I deliberately choose to challenge my students with the proposition that it *was* that bad—and worse. I tell them I'm going to draw stark pictures, and use shocking stories, and employ the most pointed logic I can devise to make that point. I tell them I intend to offer not only a short, intellectual education about what happens in the families of abusers, but an emotional one as well. I tell them I intend to get a rise out of them (anger, fear, revulsion, or resistance), and when I do, I shall consider that I've done my job. And what's more, I tell them that if they find themselves going through emotional upheaval of some sort as the course progresses, they're responsible for their own feelings; I'm not.

The class proceeds, and the pressure begins to grow. Usually, about the fifth or sixth week of the session, when we begin to explore the kinds of sexual battering children of alcoholic families have to endure, all hell breaks loose. (Talking about sex can do that.) Some cry, one or two might disappear permanently from class, and invariably I will be attacked for the inadequacy of the approach I'm employing to show why such abuse almost inevitably happens in the families of the chemically dependent.

All of a sudden, the name of the game is "uproar," yet the students don't even know they're in uproar to avoid their memories and their pain.

This academic mayhem only underscores the point I'm raising with them. I plainly told them what I was going to do before I did it; I reminded them of what I was doing as I did it; and I explained what had happened after I'd done it. And yet . . . uproar. Inescapably, they have become *emotionally* aware of the intense power of their childhood programming and are no longer able to examine their defenses dispassionately or academically. All of a sudden, it's that bad . . . again.

I am going to presume that what is true for my class is true for you: You didn't pick up this book by accident. I want to take you through the story, as I do with my students, step by step, with no surprises. At the end, after we've examined the acts, the emotional issues, and the survival strategies of ACOAs, let your own gut tell you whether it was that bad. Remember: Just like my students, you may find yourself being angry, getting annoyed, or eager to prove that I'm nuts. And as I tell my students, be responsible for your feelings.

Back to Basics

In Psychology 101, I learned that good attention is better than bad attention, and bad attention is better than no attention. Loki reinstructed me in that maxim when he was a puppy. If I needed to discipline him, his obvious "druthers" were that I scold or shake him rather than exile him to the back porch. That banishment was the ultimate punishment, the ultimate abuse. Yet the one abuse that's inevitably, invariably, and absolutely guaranteed to occur in families of chemical abusers is the worst abuse of no attention. Children of abusers begin on the bottom.

The plot is usually some variation of the following: Baby gets born and comes home from the hospital, and at first—for about the first three months of life—receives pretty much the love and attention babies need. But then, as baby's novelty wears off, as 3:00 A.M. feedings, Pamper-pooping, and colic start to take their toll, Mommy's and Daddy's preexisting attitudes and habits begin to reassert themselves; they actually begin to betray their child by withdrawing their love. Why? In plainest terms: because Mommy and Daddy have never been a match for their chemicals. It's as though the chemicals reassert their claim to their subjects, and Mommy and Daddy can do nothing but betray their child, withdrawing their love and regiving their focus to their addiction—in spite of themselves.[1]

Numbed-Out Mommies and Daddies

"Psychology's no match for chemistry," my psychiatrist in treatment used to say. And if one or both of baby's parents are chemical abusers, there are chemical realities that necessarily will hold sway, despite all Mommy's and Daddy's best intentions and ideas about parenting. Chemical abusers' feelings are, at the very least, chemically distorted, especially if the drug of choice is alcohol or some other "downer," like Valium.

When I was doing my drinking, I couldn't feel. I was shut down emotionally; alcohol is a chemical depressant, and chemical depressants depress. To put it another way, I was chemically blocked from being emotionally present to myself. If I can't be emotionally present to myself, there's no way I can be emotionally present to someone else. Likewise, the flat chemical fact is that chemically addicted

[1] Another element in Mommy's and Daddy's quick disillusionment about parenting can be—if the mother is the alcoholic—that the child is the victim of "Fetal Alcohol Syndrome." Such infant "alcoholics" can be difficult to deal with, and the mother's guilt feelings about the child's condition may be potent—both reasons for returning to the oblivion of the bottle. Cf. Michael Dorris's *The Broken Cord* (New York: Harper and Row, 1989).

parents literally cannot be emotionally attuned and attentive to their children because they cannot be emotionally tuned into themselves.

Likewise for codependent parents. The universal emotional symptom of codependency is depression. How else, other than by shutting down emotionally (depressing), could a codependent possibly stay with an abuser? Denial lived out emotionally is depression—and codependents are nothing if not in denial.

Abusers and codependents can be temporarily jolted out of their depressions by events like the birth of a baby. But, like water seeking its own level, if they remain chemically abusive and codependent, they will soon fall back into their depressions and emotional distortions. It cannot be otherwise; psychology is no match for chemistry. If you don't believe that, try "deciding" to stay awake after a doctor gives you a general anesthetic prior to an operation.

Back to baby. It gets born, responded to, and loved for a short while (it's new and exciting, after all). Then Mommy and Daddy do their chemical and codependent things. As surely as day follows night, sooner or later baby gets betrayed by being emotionally abandoned—big time! The child may continue to receive physical nurturing; food, clothing, and shelter. But on the emotional level, it gets only minimal attention—and even that is usually "negative." From almost the very beginning, then, a child in a chemically abusive family is guaranteed the worst kind of abuse. It *cannot* be otherwise.

Kids, even infants, are amazingly tough. They can endure starvation, homelessness, even beatings, and still survive. They will die, though, if they get no attention. (If you find this hard to believe, check it out with any pediatric nurse.) And the children know it—intuitively, in their guts, they know it. Getting attention is literally a matter of life and death for them, far more primary than getting food or shelter.

Those are the bare-bones facts of an infant's earliest emotional life. The legacy these parents bequeath to their children are two issues that will dominate their feeling lives for the rest of their days: betrayal and abandonment. From then on, these children *expect* to be betrayed and abandoned by those they love; for if Mommy and

Daddy "loved" them in that way (Mommy and Daddy *can't* be wrong), being betrayed and being abandoned is what love is all about.

Like Parent, Like Child

Little kids are smart and quick: the earlier the lesson, the deeper the impact. For the children of chemically dependent families, the experience of love, from the very beginning, is about threat and death rather than nurture and life. Perhaps more than any other group of people, ACOAs intuitively grasp the meaning of the title I've given this book. The theme song of their lives is "The Opposite of Everything Is True"—to "love" and "be loved" is to be abused and then die.

To my knowledge, my father was not an alcoholic, but he did "abandon" me four months after I was born. He died unexpectedly of a heart attack. My mother tells me he was a good father; we had bonded deeply by the time he dropped dead at the wheel of his truck. Years later, when I was four years sober, a forty-two-year-old man, I was driving through California while on vacation with a close friend. The preceding months had been extremely tough; I'd been going through tremendous turmoil while deciding whether or not to resign from the priesthood. I felt exhausted, empty, confused, isolated. More than anything else, I wanted my friend to hold me and let me cry. But I could not ask for what I wanted; my mouth would not let the words out.

For a day and a half, as we drove, I struggled to ask him for what I wanted. At last, when I croaked out my desire to him, I went through one of the most upsetting emotional experiences I've ever undergone. It was as though speaking the words about what I wanted caused me to be jolted and stunned by a bolt of lightning. For close to twenty-four hours afterward, I was disoriented and in shock. My friend had to lead me around by the hand, put me to bed, and almost had to feed me by hand.

As I processed those traumatic hours in my Twelve-Step programs and therapy, the experience began to make sense. As when I was a newborn infant, I needed and wanted nurturing affection from a man I loved. But when I asked my friend to hold me, suddenly, almost explosively, I relived the trauma I'd undergone when the first man I'd ever loved, my father, abandoned me. When he died, I must have shut down in automatic self-defense, for I am sure that the full intensity of those feelings would have killed a baby. It was my first lesson in the "game" called "I Love You, Good-bye."

Compared to the experiences of children in alcoholic and addicted families, and despite its pain, what I went through was fairly clean and simple. What those children have to deal with is the traumatic confusion of parents who are "there" but "not there." Most of their mommies and daddies don't die or leave. Physically, they're present and accounted for; emotionally, they've vanished. What's a baby to do when his head tells him one thing and his heart tells him another?

What If Mommy's Name Were "God"?

Babies can resolve that confusion in only one way. Since they are so totally dependent upon their parents for their very survival, they *have* to believe their heads instead of their hearts; they have to believe what they see instead of what they feel. They have to choose to believe that Mommy and Daddy are "there." Thus, these children, from their infancy, have to make a decision that will both guide and devastate their emotional lives henceforth: Their hearts and their feelings cannot be trusted, they don't count. The emotional die has been cast.

Notice that we haven't even begun to look at two other factors that the children of abusive families usually undergo: the parallel progressions of their parents' chemical dependency and codependency, along with the abusive, battering attention by which their parents almost always victimize them. Again, there's a paradox. These children do start on the bottom, as it were, but it gets worse.

Chemical dependency is progressive; so is codependency. Chemical abusers and codependents always get worse, not better. Consequently, the degree of emotional withdrawal, emotional "nonpresence," the child must suffer from its parents inevitably gets greater and greater.

In and of itself, that fact is cruel enough. But the cruelty is compounded. Children need, demand, fight for, attention—good attention if possible, bad attention if the only other option is no attention. Thus, those who survive—that is, those who don't go insane or die—are the ones who've somehow got some sort of attention. It's a simple matter of life or death, and the child knows it. Of course, they (we) don't reason it all out; they (we) just know it in the gut, instinctively. And so we children, the babies, set out to get attention. The irony is that we seek attention from the very people who have already betrayed our trust by withdrawing their attention in the first place.

Children have to believe with every fiber of their beings that Mommy and Daddy love them. They believe it even when all the evidence is to the contrary. Life itself depends on that belief, and so children must interpret any expression of attention Mommy or Daddy deign to give them as a sign of care and nurture, as a sign of love.

The implications here are frightening and (more honestly) disgusting. The children have no alternative but to suppose that their parents' emotional withdrawal is somehow a sign of love. This is their first lesson in the opposite of everything being true. To survive, these children must come to see that the heart of being loved is being abandoned. To survive, they must embark on their personal lifestyle of denial.

This lesson can only be reinforced as the parents continue to practice and progress in their mutual diseases. The children devise ways to get the attention they need, and it works. As Mommy and Daddy get sicker, however, these manipulations stop working. So the children get more manipulative, ever more skillful at wheedling what they need (in religion, that's called *prayer*). And again, it works until it doesn't. The cycle repeats and repeats; the manipulation becomes more habitual and skilled; the denial deepens. It's repulsively predictable.

And what of the physical beatings and the verbal character assassinations, the whippings and mockery, the tangible and bleeding hurts of so many families scarred by chemical abuse? The mold has already been set. Bad attention is better than no attention; besides, the beatings come from Mommy and Daddy—so, despite the hateful pain, "I must deserve it." They must be signs of love. It's as if every child in these families must say, "I cannot trust them. I always have to be on guard. Yet the very fact that they're here to be on guard against assures me that they *do* love me, because that means they haven't abandoned me. At least there's someone here."

I once read a newspaper story about Joseph Stalin. Some of his cronies were questioning the old dictator about the secret of power. He replied by acting out a parable. He had one of his bodyguards fetch a live chicken. He held the bird with one hand and plucked out all its feathers with the other as his "friends" watched in horror. Then he dropped the bird to the ground. Instead of running off, the crazed, denuded chicken leaned against Stalin's leg, staring up at him with terror—and adoration. Stalin eyed the men about him and said, "That's the meaning of power." That, too, I suggest, is the meaning of a child's life in the chemically abusive family. I told you; it is that bad.

The Battle Hymn of the Confused

To the degree and depth Mommy and Daddy practice their chemical and emotional dependencies, they are incapable of loving themselves, much less their offspring.

That's a fact, but it's a fact the children literally cannot accept. For they have to survive (the deepest drive of any living being), and yet—to survive—they have to believe Mommy and Daddy love them. So, these children have no choice but to go into denial. That's the first step of their strategy, the unreal but totally powerful belief that undergirds all that follows.

Next, in spite of that belief that their parents love them, they have experienced that Mommy and Daddy can't be trusted. So, bending logic before that overarching need to survive, they have to choose always to be on guard (to be paranoid) against the ones whom they cannot doubt love them.

The last step then falls into place. Children always believe they're responsible for Mommy's and Daddy's feelings. "So, if they reject me, it must be my fault, not theirs. From here on out, then, I won't ever give them reason to reject me again; I'll be exactly who they want me to be." In short, the children choose to become manipulators of their parents' feelings. People-pleasing Mommy and Daddy into giving them the kind of attention they need is their only hope of survival.

If (as an adult) you think all that's confusing, try putting yourself in the kids' shoes!

Thus we come to the battle plans, the tactics through which children implement their people-pleasing strategies of constant wariness and survival. Which tactic a child chooses most often depends on two factors, how many brothers and sisters it has, and where it comes in the birth order. (When you're a baby, your options *are* limited.) The success of the chosen tactics is measured against the goals of the operation, namely, getting "good" attention and avoiding battering by pleasing Mommy and Daddy.

Mommy and Daddy are, of course, the pivotal figures, because the name of the game is "To Become What They Want Me to Be"—always and everywhere. Nothing else counts. Because it is a matter of survival—life or death—mere excellence is not good enough. Only perfection wins this contest.

Dramatis Personae

So each of the children in a chemically dependent family plays a role, an acted-out manipulation that may or may not have much to do with who they really are, but has everything to do with who their parents want them to be.

Nearly always, these roles are based on half-truth. Even in the midst of the practice of their diseases, most abusers and codependents are not so far under the influence or so deeply depressed that they cannot see the obvious in their children. It would be rather difficult not to notice that one's firstborn is one's firstborn; or that a personable child is personable; or that a quiet child is quiet; or that a beautiful child is beautiful. I may not have been privy to what was occurring in a person's depths, but even at my drunkest, I could react to some degree to what I could see.

So Mommy and Daddy see what they can see, and they respond to what they like in the child. The rest they ignore or batter or misinterpret. For example, they may see that their child is intelligent: They give positive strokes to the kid for being smart, yet they are unconcerned about and ignore what he's smart about. They have no concern about his interests.

Children are not stupid; they catch on quickly: ". . . what Mommy and Daddy like, I should be, I must be. What they don't like or can't see only gets me battered or ignored. Thus, those parts of me they reject and to which they turn a deaf ear (usually such minor items as my personal wants, likes, desires, and feelings) are bad—life-threatening, in fact." That's an equation so easy even an infant can put it together . . . and all too many have.

There are four basic roles or manipulations children act out— and a nearly infinite number of variations on how they can be played. Let's look at a quick, general sketch of each of them to get a more concrete picture of how the game is played.

The Hero (Usually the Oldest Child)

Being the firstborn, of itself, makes you special, but at a price. If your name is Windsor, for example, it could make you king or queen of England; but you'd never really have a life of your own. In spite of his responsibilities, however, Prince Charles is still more free than the crown prince or princess in a chemically dependent home. If Charles so chooses, he *can* abdicate; firstborn children of alcoholics and addicts never get that option.

Just because they are the firstborn, they become the living repositories of their parents' hopes and dreams. That's true for most first-borns in most families—healthy as well as unhealthy. But in abusers' families, heroes and heroines face the crushing demand that they assume responsibility for the affairs of state by the time they're four or five years old (and sometimes even earlier). Even Charles got to wait until his thirties before they officially crowned him Prince of Wales.

It's not uncommon in families of the chemically dependent that a little five- or six-year-old eldest child cooks for the rest of the family, does the laundry, disciplines the younger kids, puts Mommy and Daddy to bed when they're drunk, and, in fact if not name, becomes the head of the household. And you can be sure that, through it all, the little heir apparent is doing a monumental self-imposed guilt trip for not knowing how to do it all better. Duty is the motto; people-pleasing the game; fear the motivation; perfection the goal.

The whole scenario makes Number One Son (or Daughter) very, very special to the parents and to the other children. But the price of that specialness is the loss of childhood, spontaneity, playfulness, and wonder. Heroes and Heroines never have the chance to be little. For them, being little, childlike, is about the most threatening state they could possibly imagine themselves experiencing.

Being little, you see, means being dependent and vulnerable, and those are precisely the two conditions firstborns from chemically abusive families are escaping by all their duty-doing and becoming "big." Their own childishness is to them the single strongest threat to their survival. Again, the equation locks into place: Being little (acting childishly) is "bad," so bad that the children actually feel guilty when they behave like the children they are. In their own eyes (and usually in the eyes of the rest of the family), they've grown up—full of wisdom, strength, endurance, courage—at the ripe old age of six and a half. No wonder they tend to be exhausted by the time they're thirty.

The only crumb eldest children get to throw to their emaciated and stunted humanity is the privilege of having a secret life. It's the emotional safety valve that preserves them from explosion. Witness Jack Kennedy's secret sexual life[2] or the eldest son/museum curator/art critic who moonlights as a professional wrestler. The com-

---

[2] I am well aware that Jack Kennedy was not the oldest child in his family by birth order. When his older brother, Joe, was killed during World War II, however, Jack "moved up" and took over the Hero role of the oldest child.

panions and associates of the eldest's public life are seldom if ever allowed to meet the denizens of this secret world. And if, by some chance toss of the dice, those two worlds do come face-to-face, the emotional price the Hero pays is at the very least acute embarrassment. (I wonder, for example, how many bigamists are the eldest children of chemically dependent families.)

I can only speculate why secret lives are so prevalent in the dysfunctional patterns of eldest-children Heroes. My guess is that they are usually born before their parents' chemical dependency and codependency have reached full bloom. In some ways, the abuse and craziness to which they're subjected are somewhat less sick than those suffered by the succeeding children (as you'll soon see). Consequently, it could be that they receive some small hint—a subtle "virus" in their "programming," as it were—that there might be other possibilities to life than just being big. The message is always so distorted and the theme is so minor that eldest children's ideas about play and fun are pretty twisted. Nonetheless, the safety valves of those "secret lives" seem to provide enough of a balance that, when coupled with the inherent demands of being big and strong, they make Heroes and Heroines hard nuts to crack. It's a commonplace among alcoholism and ACOA professionals that doctors, lawyers, clergy, and other therapists are the most resistant to any healing process—and I dare you to find a more ready-made group of Heroes and Heroines (usually from chemically dependent and/or dysfunctional families) than these professionals.

The Middle Children

As middle children develop their survival strategies, they have to factor in their brothers and sisters as well as Mommy and Daddy. And the first thing they learn is that *they can't compete.* Firstborn children are older, are bigger, are the crown princes or princesses and, therefore, will receive all the attention, honors, and accolades that are their due. The youngest is always the "baby." The second and third children may eventually turn out smarter, bigger, more talented, and richer human beings than the oldest, or cuter and more winsome than the youngest; but for all of that, they cannot change the fact that the firstborn is the firstborn and the lastborn is the baby.

As the survival strategies of middle children are dictated by their being in the middle, they have to manipulate from their parents whatever attention might be left over after the firstborn and lastborn have received their due. Considering Mommy's and Daddy's stunted capabilities, that's a challenge. Consequently, in chemically abusive homes, it's guerrilla warfare all day, every day. No wonder authors like Wayne Kritsberg diagnose ACOAs to be suffering from post-traumatic shock syndrome, just like Vietnam veterans![3]

The Scapegoat (Usually the Second Child)

If the eldest child gets attention by being responsible, the middle child Scapegoat gets it by being irresponsible. If the Hero-Crown Prince gets noticed for being good, the Scapegoat gets it by being bad. At least, that's what it looks like on the surface. The actual dynamics of the Scapegoat's role are more subtle, however.

Once a year in ancient Israel, the high priest would pick a black goat from among the animals offered for sacrifice. The people of Jerusalem would file into the temple, and each would lay hands on the goat. That action symbolized that they were laying the guilt for their sins on the animal. Then the goat was driven out into the desert to starve to death, and with it went the people's guilt.

The best descriptive definition of guilt I've ever heard is that it's ". . . living out somebody else's anger." In the *danse macabre* of chemically abusive families, one emotion above all others energizes and, at the same time, corrodes the interconnections of all its members: anger. Anger flows from fear, and there is nothing more fearful than to live a life totally dependent on a chemical, or on another human being, or on parents who can't really care. Yet, if there is one emotion about which the members of chemically abusive families must be in denial, it is anger. For if we *knew* how angry we were, we'd then know how scared we were. But if we knew how

---

[3]Wayne Kritsberg, *The Adult Children of Alcoholics Syndrome* (New York: Bantam Books, 1985), Chapter 7.

scared we were, we'd probably have to start telling the truth about our lives.

Thus, the anger is always there inside the chemically abusive family, boiling and churning, like liquid in a pressure cooker. Like a pressure cooker, alcoholic and addicted families need a safety valve. Hence, the Scapegoat.

In spite of its negative appearance, being a Scapegoat is a positive, caretaking service to the family. If our Scapegoat is there to be angry, then we can stay calm. If our Scapegoat is there to be guilty, then we can be innocent and good—and so not need to change. If our little Hero or Heroine is the embodiment of our hopes and pride, our Scapegoat is the "sacrament" of our darker, broken sides. By having a Hero to embody their dreams, parents can stay in denial of their own failures; by having a Scapegoat to blame, they can affirm their own righteousness.

Thus, for all of the worry and hurt parents go through about the rages and escapades of their Scapegoats, they are emotionally invested in keeping their Scapegoats just that—Scapegoats. For all of his hell-raising and acted-out rage, the Scapegoat is still, in a very subtle way, "people-pleasing" his mommy and daddy. Without him, the constantly rumbling pressure of their own anger and denial might breech their inner defenses—and if that happened, they might have to change. In short, once a set of parents has gone through all the work of begetting, programming, and training a well-functioning Scapegoat, it would be a great disservice to their mutual denial systems if their errant child were to mend his ways.

The Lost Child (Usually the Third)

Like the Scapegoat, the Lost Child has to deal not only with the parents but also one specific sibling. The joker in the Scapegoat's deck is the eldest-child/Hero; for the Lost Child, it's the lastborn/ Mascot.

Fundamentally, the Lost Child is a displaced person. When he was born, he was the youngest and, as such, had a role ready-made, just waiting for him to come along and assume it. By the time he arrived, the roles of Hero and Anti-hero (Scapegoat) were filled;

the "adult" niches were taken, and so the only "logical" thing for him to do was to stay professionally little, be the "baby of the family," the Mascot. But then he got dealt a cruel twist: Mommy and Daddy had another baby. The attention that used to be his now went to another.

If the former Mascot protests too loudly in the chemically abusive family, he can be assured of one definite reaction from his parents, some variation on "Shut up, kid, or you'll get something to cry about." He has no choice but to recede into the background and be a "good [read: quiet] little child." There may be some strokes available for not causing any trouble.

Because Lost Children are lost, their role is the most difficult to describe. It's like trying to talk about the inner workings of a hole. The great facility of the Lost Child is to disappear—at the very least emotionally, and often physically. They have the uncanny ability to intuit trouble and family blow-ups hours before they occur. By the time the storm strikes, they've already had their hatches battened down and their fallout shelters stocked and locked from the inside. Their greatest skill is blending in to the point of not being noticed.

But if ever there was a living example of the opposite being true, it's the Lost Child. The key to understanding this child's inner life is to realize that he's been displaced and betrayed. He is not a happy camper, but to survive he dare not let even himself, much less Mommy and Daddy, know the depth of his angry resentment. There is a slowly building volcano in the Lost Child's depths. God help the people in the vicinity when finally he blows.

The Lost Child will be invisible, self-effacing, quiet. That's what Mommy and Daddy want; that's what they will get—in spades. He will do as he is told; he will help when it's needed; in adulthood, he may be the bachelor son who stays at home until he is in his late fifties to take care of his bedridden mother. People might see the quiet, good things he does, but seldom will they be able even to glimpse what's happening in his heart; if they do, they'll wish they hadn't.

The Mascot (Usually the Youngest)

Mascots are cute. They're fun; they keep us laughing; they're the "babies of the family."

What the Hero is, the Mascot isn't; what the Hero isn't, the Mascot is. Nevertheless, Heroes and Mascots are alike in that both roles have exactly the same purpose and goal. Both of them play out their scripts to defend themselves against bad attention and no attention by controlling the ways their parents react to them. In military terms, the roles of Hero and Mascot are variations on a strategy that could be called "the emotional preemptive strike." The Hero (by being adult, big, and heroic) and the Mascot (by being childish, little, and cute) are doing their damnedest to defang Mommy and Daddy's anger before it gets a chance to get triggered. Who could get angry at someone who takes care of everyone else and always does the right thing? Likewise, how could we ever think of punishing a cute little baby who always makes us smile?

In truth, Heroes and Mascots live in a state of reactive paranoia, always waiting for the other shoe to drop. Neither of them can trust.

If the Hero longs above all else for the chance to be little and play, the Mascot wants more than anything to be taken seriously. The opposite is true.

Marilyn Monroe personified the perfect Mascot: cute, childlike, seductive—even in her suicidal death longing for respect, yet unable to believe the true seriousness with which she was loved by those two quintessential Heroes, Arthur Miller and Joe DiMaggio.

The Virtuoso (The Only Child)

The key words in describing the only child in a chemically dependent family are *special* and *alone*. There is good attention, there is bad attention, and then there's too much attention. Living under a microscope tends to make one self-conscious. Precisely because the Virtuoso is the only child, the attention he receives from his parents is undivided and uniquely focused. There's no relief as there is in families with more than one child. In those families, the kids can "spell" each other and reinforce one another as they try to deal with Mommy and Daddy.

Not so in the single-child home; alone and unsupported, the Virtuoso has to manage against and survive his parents' dysfunction. Because he is, in himself, both the oldest and youngest, he has to develop, as it were, a "double major" in role-playing; he has to be a Hero-Mascot. (Never mind the self-contradictory nature of such a demand.) Likewise, he has to develop a "double minor" in Scapegoating and Getting Lost. Somebody has to be the pressure valve to bleed off some of the intensity of Mommy and Daddy's denial and suppressed anger. And, as well, he has to learn to sit on his own anger (as well as any other "unacceptable" emotions he might feel); he has to become paranoid enough to efface himself well in advance of impending parental explosions.

Kids in any family always feel responsible for Mommy and Daddy's feelings. But, again, because the Virtuoso is an only child, he inevitably feels *totally* responsible for his parents' emotional life. Consequently, he sees himself to be responsible for their emotional dysfunction—all by himself, unsupported by brothers or sisters. When his parents feel guilty about mistreating him, he must become responsible for their feelings. That's a hell of a lot of guilt.

Yet, for all of the impossible and contradictory demands imposed on him, despite the bottomless confusion he must experience daily, the "Only" will project a serene and special kind of self-possession, for all by himself he has survived and pulled it off; he's done the impossible. Inside, he may be the most terrified and confused of all, but on the outside, all we lesser mortals can see is strength and the kind of independence that needs the counsel of no other person. The opposite of everything is true.[4]

[4]With regard to these roles and the birth order in which they occur: The *usual* order is as discussed; however, it may change given the unique circumstances of individual families. For an especially clear example, if the parents have focused on having a son but their first child is a daughter, when a son *is* born the firstborn girl may be shunted out of her rightful status as Heroine and find herself suddenly the Scapegoat . . . to make room at "the top" for her brother.

The Grand Finale

Some summary thoughts about the children of chemically abusive families and the roles they play . . .

Like "Uncle Joe" Stalin and his chicken, chemically abusive and codependent parents systematically pluck out of their children any sense they might have of owning their own lives, any unconditioned sense of self-worth, any belief that their lives have meaning and value of themselves. Instead of security, these parents beget paranoia. They force from their children total focus, almost adoration.

First and foremost, by giving no attention, as well as by practicing whatever abusive attention their dependencies elicit, chemically abusive parents force their kids into survival mode—all day, every day. I cannot emphasize this point too strongly: for the children, life and death in the chemically abusive family hang by a frayed and precarious thread.

Thus, to these children, the importance of their roles: By living out their roles, they survive. Their skill at their roles is simply a matter of life or death. This is their most fundamental belief: "If I am to survive, I must be the Hero (or the Scapegoat; or the Lost Child; or the Mascot) twenty-four hours a day—and I cannot be anything else." It's the black-and-white totalistic thinking of a child.

In other words, the children become as dependent on their roles as chemical dependents do on their drug of choice, or codependents do on their abusers. If you threaten their roles, they feel exactly the same way their parents do when their drug supply or relationships get threatened, *as if they're going to die.* To survive, the children have to become addicts—to a role, an image, instead of a drug or another person. The children have to believe in their roles as much as chemical abusers believe in their drugs or as codependents believe in their "love." These roles must become the be-all and end-all of the children's lives—performances of Academy Award caliber, so convincingly portrayed that the actor believes in them just as much as the audience.

Yet, for all that perfection, we're back to belief systems of denial, for as with the codependent, so with the children: *It's all a con.* A three-year-old child is a three-year-old child, not an all-wise knight in shining armor, or the incarnation of anger, or a ghostly presence floating about the corners of a room, or merely a cute little gurgling toy. I may have been the consummate actor and got into my role so totally that both my audience and I believed in the character I portrayed. I may have altered their sense of reality as well as my own. Nonetheless, it was still an act; I was still a child.

A final point: Chemical abusers are addicted to chemicals, yet chemicals are not the point of their addiction. Codependents are addicted to their abusers, yet their abusers are not the point of their addiction. Likewise, the same paradox holds for the children: They are addicted to their roles, yet their specific roles are not the point of their addiction.

This shows up graphically when one of the children in the family—say the eldest, for example—dies or goes away. The others just move up a notch. Suddenly, the Scapegoat starts behaving like a Hero, and the Lost Child becomes the Scapegoat. It's not so much *the* role I played as that I *had* a role to play. It's not *how* I survived, it's that I *did* survive.

As with the chemical dependent and the codependent, so with the child: The addiction is fundamentally empty. The point of the addiction is the addict*ing;* the point of survival is the surviv*ing;* the action becomes the end in itself.

The action of addicting is a cover-up, a continually applied anesthetic whose numbing action becomes so habitual that it takes on a life of its own. Like a flywheel gone out of control, it spins on and on, wearing down the machinery, stopping only when everything is destroyed. Eventually, addictions kill.

But better to die of something than of nothing. That's the alternative for the children. Their parents have stolen any sense they might have had of themselves. So, if the children do not have their addicting, their roles, they have nothing.

Yes. It was that bad.

Chapter 5

And It Gets Worse

Four ACOA Issues:

1. Boundaries and Limits
2. Sexual Power Plays
3. Guilt
4. Addiction to Excitement

Besides Loki, my home is graced and gentled by another presence, petite and regal. Princess is a small white cat with one blue, one green eye. She's delicate, fastidious, beautiful, and totally feminine. Loki believes her to be *his* pet and buddy, but she—while acquiescing with some reserve to the "buddy" part—definitely has different ideas about who belongs to whom, as well as which one of us three has the divine right to reign over the other two.

Right before Christmas of 1988, she had her first litter. She did a nice, sensible job of it, as one of my feline-fancying clients pointed out—only three kittens, two of them white with black spots on the tops of their heads and one black-striped tabby (a dead giveaway about which of the neighborhood toms was the daddy).

She whelped them in my bedroom closet Saturday morning, shortly before I woke. The alarm went off; I sat up in bed. A questioning meow echoed from out of the closet; and she followed it, jumping up on the bed with a bewildered look on her face and a tummy decidedly smaller than it had been the evening before. We traded stares for a moment. Then she jumped down and ran into the living room. I got down on my hands and knees to search the closet corners, and I found the tiny, naked newborns, still wet and already squeaking their hunger. I transferred them to the box a friend had helped me ready the week before and put Princess in with them. At first she didn't know what to do, so I laid her on her side and put the babies to her nipples. They began to suckle, and then she relaxed and started to purr—as if she'd suddenly realized, "Ahh . . . so that's what this program's all about." I'm still awed at how in an instant that ordinary cardboard box became so luminously sacred.

After three or four days, Loki got to meet the kittens. Despite my fears, Princess didn't object to his nuzzling and licking them, and he seemed to enjoy playing uncle. He was carefully gentle with his affection, and she trusted him.

Later that week, though, it was a different story. A friend and client who sometimes brings his dog to play with Loki while we're in session walked in with Gray Eyes in tow. Gray Eyes is as big as Loki, and just as gentle. His human (my client) was unaware of the kittens' birth, and I was unaware that Gray Eyes was coming along to this particular session.

They came in together. Loki woofed a welcome, and Princess looked up over the edge of the nursery box. She may weigh five pounds sopping wet, but in the second she spotted Gray Eyes, she expanded to three times her normal size and became as fierce as a cornered leopard. She simply flew: By herself, she had that poor dog surrounded. I reached in to grab her—like a good ACOA, caretaking fool—and she almost took off the tip of one of my fingers. Luckily, we got Gray Eyes out the door before any other blood got spilled. Slowly, Princess calmed down, but—growling—she stalked the perimeter of her babies' box for a good half hour, spitting at anyone who even dared to look in her direction.

Like Loki, Princess is and does as her genes and breeding would have her be and do. It was fascinating to watch her mother her litter. She fed them and protected them. She groomed them and gathered them into the curl of her body at night. She mourned them when it was time, after ten weeks, for them to leave for their new homes. But once they were gone, that was that. When Sydney, the biggest of the kittens, came back with his humans for a visit a month later, Princess hissed and nearly ran him out of the house for trespassing on her territory.

She knows how to love, but she also knows how to let go. She lives her life in the here and now, with no fear or regrets about yesterday or dread of tomorrow. She's the perfect parent for a functional feline family. When her kits are grown, they won't have to deal with the emotional scars and warpings the human offspring of alcoholic/dysfunctional families must confront.

In Chapter 4, we looked at what happened to those human kids, at the traumas they undergo, and the coping strategies they develop as a result of living in a chemically abusive family. As a family portrait, this picture has been anything but flattering.

This chapter presents a different (though equally ugly) kind of picture. In order to illustrate what happens to us children when we grow up, let's discuss four specific problems that commonly raise their heads in our adulthoods. There's nothing sacrosanct about the number *four,* nor is there anything sacred about the particular issues I've chosen. I've selected these four as "case studies" simply because they're the ones I find myself dealing with over and over again; and because, in my client population, they're the issues that seem to occur most often.

Try them on and see if they ruffle your emotional feathers a bit.

I. Boundaries and Limits

Princess has no difficulty setting or enforcing boundaries. She doesn't second-guess her fear or her anger, nor does she guiltily question whether she overreacted to a situation. She doesn't carry the burden of "shoulds," "ought-to's," and "rights and wrongs" that we humans shoulder on a daily basis. "Appropriateness" does not concern her.

She gives her affection by choice rather than compulsion—at least, so it looks—and suspends it with equal "freedom." She goes with her intuition about the danger or benignity of a situation, and above all else, she never, never loses her self-possession or her ability to respond to her feelings.

Existential psychologists tell us there are two kinds of fear, a healthy one that energizes us for self-protection and a "neurotic" kind that paralyzes us in the face of danger. A healthy person walking down a jungle path can take off like a world-class sprinter when he rounds a bend and comes face-to-face with a hungry tiger. But the neurotic who chances upon the same tiger is so rooted in place by his fear that he's likely to go catatonic (literally unable to run, unable to distance himself) as the cat ambles up to begin munching. Blandly put, he has no ability to set boundaries and thus protect himself.

We ACOAs tend to be case studies in the latter category of fear. In childhood, I got the message, from my addictive stepfather, "Shut up, kid, or you'll get something to cry about!" I learned quickly that he meant what he said, and so, equally as quickly, honed my ability to stifle my tears and fear. Since even something so minor as a pouty look got the same parental reaction, I soon learned that no expression whatsoever of grief or pain was allowable. "Stuffing it" became my automatic reaction and practice.

Likewise for laughter: Addicts and alcoholics are paranoid; they "know" whom their children are laughing at. So anything louder than a muted giggle didn't "wash" during childhood: It was too dangerous.

It's obscene enough that parents would disallow their children the opportunity to experience and express their feelings at any time, but the far uglier travesty was that they forced us to begin and to practice emotional muteness habitually, as a lifestyle. In short order, most of us became self-policing. Masters as we are of the emotional preemptive strike, we learned to disallow ourselves the feeling and expression of those emotions Mommy and Daddy didn't like. That way, we not only pleased them but also beat them at their own game by denying them the chance to get angry at us. Mao would love us: We won militarily by co-opting them on their own ground, and we won politically by coming out of the fray looking like the good guys.

That skill at emotional guerrilla warfare was absolutely necessary to our survival in childhood. But there's a slight problem with it once we become adults . . . the war's over. In fact, we won it simply by surviving to adulthood. But like punch-drunk fighters who can't hear the bell, we keep on swinging and ducking . . . ducking and swinging.

But, remember: Unlike boxers, we've learned to punch by holding back, and win by emotionally evaporating. The unforgivable tactical error was to stand up fully visible, honestly expressing and sharing our feelings, making ourselves emotionally vulnerable to the acceptance—or rejection—of others.

As adults, most of us probably find ourselves relating in friendship and love with chemical abusers, codependents, and other ACOAs. Popular myth to the contrary, emotional "like" is attracted to emotional "like," because we most easily and naturally relate to the kind of people with whom we have been trained to relate, namely the members of the first community to which we belonged, our family. That fact strands us in a fascinating emotional pickle: The closer we ACOAs get to those we come to like and love, the more we find ourselves becoming emotionally unavailable and defensed.

To survive in their families, they had to become so paranoid, so alert to others, that they became almost able to read their parents' minds. So did we. ACOAs are hypersensitive: We can scope out a blow-up three days ahead of time; we have a sixth sense for danger and threat. The more vulnerable we were to somebody—Mommy and Daddy, for example—the more attuned to and paranoid about their moods we had to be.

But for all of that, mind reading remains an "almost" rather than an accomplished skill. We're good at it, but we're not divine; we can't do it perfectly all of the time. Besides, this kind of paranoia is like the arms race: The better you become at sniffing me out and deciphering the defenses I've deployed around my feelings, the more sophisticated I'm going to get at blotting out the traces of my emotional hiding places. It's a programmed-in, progressive, automatic process. Being vulnerable just isn't an acceptable option; experience has taught me it's too dangerous.

Between a Rock and a Hard Place

The consequences of this emotional "two-step" to a relationship are murderous. If those we love can't experience where we hurt, or why we laugh, or what words scrape our feelings raw, how can they know how to care for or love us? How can they know our boundaries or our limits? And since they are in the same boat, how can we know theirs?

Even more, if we have become so skilled at emotional nonexpression, how can we know our own boundaries and limits? We humans come to know ourselves, define ourselves, by bouncing up against others. I do not know the pain of burning until I have touched the fire; I do not know the joy of love until I've fallen for someone; I do not know the surge of anger without an enemy. How do I even really know my own name unless there was somebody to christen me, somebody to address me by it? How can I have a language unless there is some other with whom I can communicate?

As well, feelings demand the completion of expression. If grief has no tears, it implodes, collapses from the inside into nothing more than flat and shriveled memories.

Alva tells a story. Two little boys are born. The first is kept inside all the time, and although he learns to read by the time he's three and tests out with a 140 IQ, he's not allowed to experience the world outside his parents' home. The second goes out to play all day, every day, and on the beach one afternoon he picks up a black rock. He feels it, and bobbles it in his hand, and tastes it, as kids do. After about an hour of playing with the stone, he tosses it in the ocean and goes on his way.

Eventually, the two boys become classmates. Their first-grade teacher decides one day to give them a test on black rocks. But she doesn't ask about "rocks"; instead they're "r-o-c-k-s"; they're "h-a-r-d" instead of "hard," "h-e-a-v-y" instead of "heavy," "b-l-a-c-k" instead of "black." One boy flunks, and the other passes with a perfect score. Which was which?

The first boy passed and pleased his teacher; from his reading and study, he *understood* all about rocks. The second boy hadn't learned to spell yet, so he flunked and ended up in the academic doghouse.

But which of the boys knew, really *knew,* what a rock was?

As for rocks, so for ourselves and with others. Until we feel and touch and play with others and with ourselves, like the second boy did with his rock, we cannot really know ourselves.

Princess never has a moment of doubt about who she is and what she's doing. She doesn't have to guess about when to purr with motherly contentment or calculate when to go berserk in protection of her litter. Healthy persons (I think there are a few) don't need to rationalize in order to give themselves permission to get angry when they're trespassed upon, nor do they need much intellectual processing before they run from a hungry tiger on the jungle trail.

But we ACOAs do. We hear childhood admonitions like "You shouldn't feel that way," and "Don't get angry with me, young lady!," and "Quit sniffling and grow up!," and "Big boys don't cry!"

Consequently, we learned to live in our heads because our hearts were declared off-limits. In our childhoods, all we could call our own were the fantasies and rationalizations we nurtured and protected in our secret minds. And to the extent we made our brains into our homes, we neither laugh nor cry, we can't celebrate or grieve, we experience neither sorrow nor joy. We were so repressed that we became depressed, without feeling. Like Alva's boy who never got outside the house to experience his world, we know how to figure things out, but we've no feel for where we end and the other begins; we have no feeling for life.

As an unnamed member of one of my therapy groups said, "Oh! You mean we're emotionally fucked!"

II. Sexual Power Plays

Of Knights and Damsels Faire . . .

If we talk of feelings and joy and if we talk about grief, we have to talk of love and sex. Lancelot and Guinevere (names changed to protect the guilty) are a couple I know. I sponsor Lancelot in AA. About five years ago, I met him sitting on the porch of the Alano Club. He was crying—not simply a tear or two, but loud, gasping sobs. I sat beside him and, once he'd calmed down, he told me what was going on.

He and Guinevere had been lovers, but several months earlier Guinevere had decided she no longer wanted to be tied down in relationship, so she left. Every so often, though, she'd show up at Lancelot's door, obviously horny and demanding a hot session in bed. Lancelot, being the good alcoholic/codependent/ACOA he is, couldn't say no, even though he always felt used and cheap afterward. And, unfortunately, he was still as sexually hooked on Guinevere as Guinevere was on him.

Just as he was leaving for the AA meeting on the day I met him, Lancelot had again found Guinevere at his door, eager for another "thump, thump" session. He'd put her off by saying he had to go to his meeting, but had promised—after a bit of pressure—to come right home afterward. He sat on the club steps crying because he felt frustrated and hurt at being used, as he said, "Like a piece of meat," yet truly unable to say no.

I don't know where it came from, but a question popped out of my mouth, "Well, *can* you be a piece of meat?"

"What do you mean?" he replied.

"Try this. Go home right after the meeting. Take a shower. Splash on some of your best cologne. Put on your sexiest cut-offs and tightest tank top. When she arrives, let her in and do your best beefcake tease for her. Ask her if you really turn her on. Don't let her touch you until she says yes and is practically drooling. Then take her into the bedroom and strip down for nooky. But, before you actually get down to business, reach over and set the alarm clock for exactly one hour. Then go to it. When the alarm goes off, even if you're in mid-ejaculation, get up, get dressed, and go out into the living room. When she follows you, tell her you're through for the evening, kiss her, pat her on the butt, and usher her out the door."

By this time, Lancelot's tears had transformed into a somewhat wicked smile. "I'll do it," he said, and ran.

The report I got back was that Guinevere was a most bewildered woman, muttering something to the effect of "I think I've been took," as she exited Lancelot's apartment a couple of hours later. For once, instead of resisting and fighting, Lance simply surrendered to Guinevere's desire. She wanted him to be a "piece of meat," nothing more. He chose to be exactly that, and she was brought face-to-face with the truth. She had lost her control over Lance, and his victory came because he no longer chose to fight against her game—to try to control her control. By playing her game on the most brutally real level, he gave up all control but regained his power, his self-respect.

Survival vs. Play

As with every other aspect of our lives, for us ACOAs sex gets subordinated to survival. It could not be otherwise. The core of our childhood trauma had to do with the betrayal of love, trust, vulnerability, and intimacy. Because the lesson of that betrayal happened so early in our lives, and because it struck so deeply to the emotional root of our beings, we tend to live with the very real expectation that anyone who professes love for us will betray us as Mommy and Daddy did. Worse, since Mommy and Daddy did the betraying and since Mommy and Daddy can't do any wrong, we expect and believe that people who love us *should* betray us. Mommy and Daddy did it that way, so, later in our lives, if somebody were to love us and yet *not* betray us, we'd have the very real suspicion their love was phony. And there's a final wicked twist: Since Mommy and Daddy are our unavoidable role models (even if we hate their guts), we've probably become expert at "loving by abandoning," too.

Thus, in the erotic arena, we tend to play the game of sex as Mommy and Daddy played the game of love with us. We had no choice but to love them and be dominated by them; what they wanted set the ground rules. We got love and attention by being pleasing to them, by manipulating them in the ways they wanted to be manipulated. We learned to set up situation after situation in such a way that they had no choice but to give us the kind of attention we wanted from them, for we did our best to leave them no choice but to be pleased with us. In short, we learned how to seduce. If they wanted cute, we gave them cute. If being "adult" got us love, we somehow grew into maturity before we were four.

Later on, when we actually do grow up and fall in love, we just transfer all those well-oiled, people-pleasing, manipulative, seductive skills. If our beloved ones want tender and sensitive, they get romanced to a *T.* If they want earthy, they get the best of our sexual technique. And it's all aimed toward one goal: to so entrap and enmesh them that they'll never be able to even think of letting go.

Since those beloved others are probably as ACOA as we, they're most likely barraging us with all their seductive skills at the same time. It can get to be quite a battle of one-upmanship, and the name of the game quickly transmutes from "Loving" to "Winning."

Loving Like Mom and Dad

The key to understanding it all is the realization that both parties in this romantic dance are so intent, so focused, on possession and control of the other that they lose ownership of themselves. Each has to become dominated by the other just as they were dominated by Mommy and Daddy—that's the *only* way to love and be loved, remember. When you look at a bare-bones outline of the situation, the self-contradictory insanity of it all comes clear: We have to be so controlling in our seductions that they have no choice but to love us as we want to be loved; yet somehow they have to be so powerful that they dominate us totally enough to do whatever they want, else we cannot believe in their love. Freud once called the process of falling in love a ". . . temporary psychosis," but this game is ridiculous.

Cats have mating rituals, but Princess—for all of her charm and beauty—never had to get that crazy to get what she wanted. She and whatever tom she connects with approach their coupling with an attitude we ACOAs can only long for—honesty.

There's another set of factors that goes into our programming about what it means to love, and it's even more depressing. Today,

I am willing to make the flat assertion that there is no such thing as an ACOA who has not been sexually abused.

The logic here is simple and unavoidable. We saw early in the last chapter how impossible it is for chemically dependent parents and their spouses to be "present" to their children's emotional development. Sexuality is an emotional phenomenon, and so here (as in all other areas of their emotional lives) the children start on the bottom—and it goes downhill from there.

Usually, most parents, even when drunk and depressed, can see the unavoidable. They can see a boy's first crop of whiskers and hear his cracking, deepening voice. They can see that their daughter is starting to develop breasts. But what's happening beneath the child's surface—the urges, feelings, questions, attractions, confusions—that's a different story. These mommies and daddies can give to their children's feeling lives no more than they can offer to their own, chemical poisoning and emotional shutdown.

Notice here that we haven't even dug into the all-too-frequent cases of incest, rape, and intended sexual shaming that so many children from chemically abusive families suffer.[1]

You see, the games of sex and love can be—indeed, should be—wonderful to play. As ACOAs, however, we have little choice but to play by the only rules we know, surviving and winning by giving no quarter. Instead of cherishing and loving, we learned to possess and abuse. Since we cannot respect ourselves, there's little chance we can respect another—even our beloved.

Equally, if we cannot love ourselves and healthily celebrate our sexuality, there's no way for us to tell or signal a partner about our truest sexual drives, sensitivities, and boundaries. Inevitably, we practice our sexual/love lives as we do the other dimensions of our lives. We never ask what our partner needs . . . that would expose our vulnerability (or our stupidity). We continue to "hope against hope" . . . because everybody knows that eventually Prince Charming will show up. We devote ourselves completely to making our

---

[1]Obviously, this is a subject much in the news today, and worth all the books and articles published about it. I pass over it quickly, but do not intend to minimize it by doing so. I hope someday to see work that highlights the full relationship of sexual abuse to chemical dependency.

partner's life work . . . because we have no value if it doesn't. We fantasize the excitement of a one-night stand into the stuff of white picket fences and fiftieth wedding anniversaries . . . because, God forbid, we must never see ourselves as human, or lusty, or anything but the embodiment of the most ideal of moral values. Lancelot and Guinevere and all their ACOA cousins by the dozens are no accident.

III. Guilt

The Double-Bind

Alva once introduced me to a prosecutor friend of his with the words, "Shirley, meet Bill. He came from one of those families." She shook my hand, laughed, and said, "Oh, so you're guilty, too." And I replied, "Yeah, if it happened and it's bad, I did it."

These days, I often envy Princess. If there's anything she's not, it's guilty or ashamed. When Gray Eyes walked in that fateful evening, those newborn kittens were not, in fact, actually threatened. There was really nothing for Princess to fear. But she didn't know that; what's more, she didn't care. It would have been nice for my ego if she'd shown any regret for mangling my fingertip, but she didn't. Instead, she simply owned her own feelings and acted accordingly. She has no inner "censor" implanted by abusive parents to pull her up short and demand she be ashamed of herself. Perhaps the most important gift she doesn't have is a bedeviling, constantly prodding doubt that questions whether she has a right to existence itself save at the pleasure and acquiescence of someone else.

Such doubts and questions are the daily lot of the ACOA. They spring from another of those insane double messages of our childhoods. On the one hand, like the kid who flunked the test (yet *knew* what the rock was), we knew with the certainty of terror that we were nothing if we did not please Mommy and Daddy.

On the other hand, like the kid who passed the test (because he *understood* what the rock was), we added it all up and came to understand that if we were careful enough, manipulative enough, seductive enough, we could control Mommy and Daddy's feelings.

In short, we came to know we were nothing, and to understand that we were everything. The one thing we could not be—either in our understanding or our knowledge—was the dependent little children we, in fact, were. We had to "do" perfect and yet "be" nothing. We couldn't even find our own truth, much less own it.

To survive, we did what anyone who lives in that kind of fear and denial must do; we obeyed orders. We gave up any sense of self-worth, for our value was totally dependent on their whim; and we came to demand of ourselves perfection in roles ordained for us by our "gods," for nothing else was allowed. In other words, we made a split in our sense of ourselves between who we were (nothing) and what we did (perfection). Who we were meant nothing; what we did meant everything.

Thus the strange phenomenon ACOAs constantly discover about themselves: We are people of huge egos about what we do, with no sense of self-respect about who we are. If someone points out that we made the wrong change for a twenty-dollar bill, we will rage indignantly at the ignorant knave, "How dare you question my honesty!" Yet we whisper within ourselves, "If they only knew the truth about me, they'd throw me in jail."

But once again, the fact is that it's all a con. Human worth—even yours and mine—is not determined by the pleasure of drunken and depressed parents. And children, no matter how gifted, determined, strong, and mature they appear, are but children, and human to boot—imperfect, thank God.

So, every time I let myself listen to that inner voice that says, "You should be ashamed of yourself," every time I exercise my ACOA need to judge myself guilty, I choose to dig myself deeper into my denial. The implication lurking behind guilt feelings is always, "I could have done/been better, if only . . ." But the core truth about addictions is that we cannot *not* do them; likewise, the bottom-line truth about "ACOAing" is that we ACOAs cannot not "ACOA." We cannot not demand perfection of ourselves, and yet, by that very demand, we perpetuate the lie of our denial and deepen the abuse.

Thus, the truth is that because we are programmed to believe, think, and behave in ACOA ways—that is, be people of denial—we do excellently at survival and horribly at life. When it comes to simple living, simply being ourselves, we are guaranteed failures because they stole from us our abilities to laugh and cry and be compassionate. We are bound to "screw it up"—to be, as Alva delicately puts it, "Lying, cheating SOBs with no self-respect."

Right now, you may be thinking, He's trying to duck responsibility for his own behavior, or He's trying to excuse his weakness. (In all honesty, there's probably even a corner of my well-tuned alcoholic/codependent/ACOA, guilt-programmed brain that's whispering the same thing.) But, " 'Tain't so." Being responsible means exactly what the word says, "able to respond." More, if that "ability to respond" is going to have any worth to our lives, it must be able to distinguish between truth and falsehood.

Living Out Somebody Else's Anger

Only when I own my truth that I am a drunk can I stop being victimized by my alcoholism; only when I do my own truth can I stop victimizing others by my chemical abuse. The same is true for my codependency and ACOA patterns. The key to being genuinely responsible is the discovery and acceptance—ownership of the *facts* of my life. Nothing else works.

And what is my "ACOA truth" that I need to see and accept if I'm going to be responsible? Just this: I am a failure at life, but I didn't program myself. I may have been following the flow of my ACOA belief system of denial for years now, always setting myself up to be a victim, abusing and victimizing others, being addicted to my role, manipulating and conning my way through life. And, as I become aware of what I'm doing, I may find I've much to grieve and make amends for. I may have many tears to cry over it all. But (and this "but" makes all the difference), those tears will be hypocritical and ultimately empty if I do not come to know that the first one for whom I need to cry is me. I must grieve for the child I was, that child who had to choose as he did and become what he was told to be . . . or die.

There's a corollary that follows from all of this—about the grandiosity of ACOA egos and their guilt. You see, if I'm guilty of all that, I must be wonderfully powerful and important. If I'm that guilty, I'm that special (of course, there's nothing an ignored, abandoned child longs for more than someday, somehow to become "that special" to someone—anyone.) It would be comical if it weren't so tragic. The guiltier I feel, the less I esteem myself; but also, the guiltier I feel, the more powerful, important, and special I can see myself to be, the bigger ego I can have. It's a dilemma, but the odds are I'll choose specialness over self-esteem any day. I don't know how to do otherwise.

The next facet of ACOA guilt I want to discuss is a doozy. The guiltier I feel about myself, the more I will blame others. We do to others what we're already doing to ourselves. That's the human way.

And the opposite is true: If I am being accepting and compassionate toward others, it can only be because I am being accepting and compassionate toward myself first. (What Christ told us in the Great Commandment of Love, "Love the Lord, your God, with all your heart . . . and your neighbor *as yourself*," was much less a command to change than a description of how we humans already do our humanity.)

Bradshaw has a term for it; he says we ACOAs live a lifestyle that's "shame-based."[2] What else could children believe when they got the message from Mommy and Daddy that they were worth only being ignored or battered? Since the belief was instilled so early in our lives, it underlies almost all we think and do and feel; it's the deepest "riverbed" guiding our course.

But, inevitably, if I constantly sit in judgment on myself, I have no choice except to do the same for everyone else. We ACOAs are infamous for our perfectionism and resentments, for our tendency ". . . not to get mad but to get even." Even those of us who play

---

[2]John Bradshaw, *Healing the Shame That Binds You* (Deerfield Beach, FL: Health Communications, 1988), and John Bradshaw, *Bradshaw On: The Family* (Deerfield Beach, FL: Health Communications, 1988).

caretaker and Hero do that: Implicitly and explicitly, we set standards and impose expectations that allow nothing less than perfection in ourselves and others. Woe betide our friends or ourselves if those standards and expectations are not met! We keep them in their place with explosions, abandonment, and passive-aggressive stabs in the back; ourselves we punish with depression, even more impossible demands, and gut-corroding guilt.

G. K. Chesterton, whom I quoted earlier, was a recovering alcoholic who possessed one attribute that's absolutely anathema to chemical dependents, codependents, and ACOAs still into the practice of their diseases: a sense of humor about himself. He loved to take ordinary sayings and turn them inside out so that their wisdom spoke once again with freshness. One of his epigrams *always* hits "emotional pay dirt," especially in ACOAs: "If it's worth doing, it's worth doing poorly."[3] When I drop that line in group-therapy sessions, the explosion is guaranteed. That it even "might" be okay for a human being *not* to do anything perfectly is a possibility anyone driven by ACOA demons finds awful to contemplate. Yet Chesterton's logic is impeccable: What's better, to live poorly or not to live; to make love poorly or not to love at all; to see the beauty of this world dimly, or not to see at all? The laugh's on us because, in our guilt and shame, about ourselves we cannot smile at all—or be gentle in the smallest way.

IV. Addiction to Excitement

Boringly Predictable

There's a fascinating phenomenon that crops up repeatedly for ACOAs in therapy. It's the rare ACOA who can go longer than a month without getting into crisis. Over the years, some of my clients have been so predictable, in fact, that I could literally plan on an increase in income at specified times during the month. The telephone would ring; they'd request an emergency session; we'd get together; they'd

---

[3]Chesterton, op. cit., p. 79.

air their issues; I'd point out the pattern once more; they'd go home; and then I'd wait for another twenty-eight and three-quarter days until they called again.

We don't know how to do quiet and peace. Nor should we. Our families of origin were not exactly sanctuaries of graciousness and equilibrium. We got programmed for trauma and uproar; we even came to long for them, and welcome them. Something's better than nothing, so crisis and battering are better than being ignored. For many of us, crisis was a genuine relief. If Daddy blew his stack or Mommy went on the rampage, at least that meant they cared enough to expend the energy. Crisis at least confirmed that we were alive and worth noticing.

So, for us, quiet, peace, tranquillity—much as we profess longing for them—are threats. They feel eerily akin to the emptiness of our first and worst abuse, being ignored. So we toss in an infidelity here and a bankruptcy there, a car accident or an exploding re-sentment, a suicidal depression or a sudden move to Timbuktu, a divorce or another marriage—just to keep the juices flowing and to avoid, at all costs, any re-echoing of the pain of childhood nothingness.

To put it another way, it seems like we are programmed to be in constant dissonance with our world, out of harmony with our environment. Princess always seems to fit, to belong right where she's at. She snoozes, perched on the couch in the sunlight, with flowing relaxation. She goes berserk in defense of her brood, but lets Loki nuzzle her kittens. She knows where she's at and lives in the present. But we ACOAs ignore today out of shame of the past or dread of the future. If we sit still too long—for over half an hour, let's say—the emptiness seems to sneak up behind us and once again start to suck us in.

Three other reasons, besides the need to avoid a repeat of child-hood emptiness, suggest themselves to me as explanations of our great need for the exciting. First, by the time we grow up, our emotional wiring has been so corroded by habitual disuse and fused by occasional overload that it takes a hell of a jolt just to get our attention. The "ordinary" doesn't have enough "kick" to even scratch our surfaces. Second, why guess at how to respond to that which we don't know (the ordinary), when our survival skills will function with automatic surefootedness in the arenas we've known since birth (the critical and the exciting)? Finally, if my childhood was a constant balancing between life and death, if survival was and is my issue, it would be surprising if, early on, I didn't develop a finely tuned ability to filter out the "nonessential"—that is, things like play, relaxation, leisure, companionship, pets, cuddling, and childish questions about why the sky is blue.

I wish I had a nickel for every time an ACOA in recovery has longed to get into relationship with a "normal person." When I'm mellow, I simply smile at the thought, but when I'm feeling cynical, I usually reply something to the effect, "If you met somebody like that, you'd get so bored in a week that you'd run away." For, you see, we're creatures of the extremes: pretty, loving, and warm won't do; for us, they have to be the *most* beautiful, the *most* warm, the *most* romantic. Orchids we can appreciate, but ordinary white daisies are little more than weeds.

The "Black Hole"

More than any other trait of our ACOA characters, our compulsive hunger for excitement bespeaks the sense of the inner emptiness lurking in the core of our beings. Because our "parental gods" did such an effective job of dismissing our emotional depths, we look within ourselves and see . . . nothing. That is what we are "supposed" to see; and so we do. Nothing drives human beings insane more quickly than nothingness. So again and again, we compulsively seek out those things which in our childhood occasionally relieved our habitual emptiness: the exciting and the traumatic.

The problem is that all too soon we become jaded and then burn out. Sooner or later, the tank runs dry; there's no energy left, no thrill unsampled. Eventually, only the "most extraordinary" can arouse a glimmer of interest. The "daily," the "ordinary," the "common," passes unnoticed and unattended. We lose any ability to live in the "here and now."

That's the worst injury, for all the great spiritual traditions teach us that the point of the journey is the journey, the point of life is living. Yet if I am so caught up in dodging the past emptiness or questing the future thrill that I continually miss the here and now, I am denying myself my own life, my own journey . . . I kill my spirit.

So, as I returned to Loki in Chapter three, I come back to Princess here. In her gracefulness and independence, she does nothing if not live her own journey. She is in harmony first of all with herself, and *precisely by being in harmony with herself,* she is in harmony with her world. If Loki teaches me about unconditional love and acceptance, she instructs me in a sense of self and self-possession. It's a wonderful education, even if overdue.

Chapter 6

What Makes the World Go Round . . . Really

"Abandon Reason, All Ye Who Enter Here"

No One Is an Island

It's become a cliché in the past decade or two that "alcoholism (read: chemical dependency) is a family disease." My sense of what people usually mean by this phrase is that once chemical users cross the line into addiction and alcoholism, their using and abusing has devastating repercussions on their families.

That understanding's correct, but there's a fuller truth that we now need to face. I'm convinced that nobody, ever, could get chemically addicted without the (at least *implied*) permission and/or support of his family or community. In other words, I'm convinced an individual can't have a belief system of denial without its being based upon and grounded in the denial of his primary support group.

In a backdoor way, I got a personal lesson in the power of social value systems when I got sober. My bottom was a two-stage affair. Stage one happened when I realized *in my head* that booze was my problem. It was a rational, intelligent process of elimination. All the props I'd employed to buttress my denial—career, status, security—were gone. My brain was left with no alternative but to admit the obvious: Booze was my problem.

But with that, things got sticky. Moments of startling clarity break through even the fog of chemical toxicity. At the moment I understood I was a drunk, my head saw with computerlike clarity that I had three choices: commit suicide, ask for help, or skip the intervening steps and go straight to Skid Road. I'd spent a good deal of time in the previous year or two contemplating suicide, and realized I couldn't do that (see the next chapter). All my education, training, and (most powerfully) my ACOA programming as an eldest only-child Hero prodded me to do the "right thing" and ask for help. My "alcoholic" wanted to go to Skid Road—yet there was one difficulty with this last alternative. Since much of my alcoholic denial was built around the fantasy that I drank with sophistication, Seattle's Skid Road—although the original of that name—was not quite classy enough. My rightful place (my grandiosity told me) was San Francisco (even when I'm sinking in my own vomit, I can be a snob). Given that concession to alcoholic elitism, number three was my option of choice.

But I couldn't scrape together even bus fare to California, and used my poverty as an excuse to employ the second option: ask for help. If the truth be told, though, even at that alcoholic bottom point I could not choose what I wanted to do over what I should do; I was powerless over my programming. The best little Hero in the world had to ask for help—and felt self-righteous about it.

The crowning glory of that self-righteousness was to request that Archbishop Hunthausen send me to Guest House, a treatment center for Catholic priests in Lake Orion, Michigan. The archbishop made the call. Then he commended me: Recalling all the priests he'd had to order, cajole, and force into treatment, he said I was the first in his experience who'd actually asked to go. I blushed modestly even as I commented to myself, "But of course!"

The Guest House driver met me at the Detroit airport. He suggested (seriously!) that we stop at the bar so I could have a final round or two: "It'll be your last chance, Father. . . ." I refused—as a good Hero should—and we hit the road for Lake Orion. It was about eleven o'clock at night, so when we got to the center, there was just me, my suitcases, and a long, empty hallway. In the second that all sank in, my alcoholic realized what my ACOA hero had done to him—and was he ever pissed! I went into a sullen, stubborn, rageful depression, and stayed there for the first seventy (or so) days at Guest House, which is why they kept me there for an extra month and a half. One denial system had steamrolled the other.

Even the denial system of my alcoholism had to yield in the face of the power of my deepest, socially programmed denial, my ACOA Hero. (As I look back and enjoy my life from its present vantage point, I guess I'm grateful to my Hero, but there's still something inside that mourns that I didn't have that last "one for the road" when I had the chance.)

Two Examples

One personal experience does not a "general rule of human behavior" make, but it does starkly demonstrate to me the power of socially sanctioned belief, even in the face of something so all-consuming as alcoholic denial. I've shared this story with many people in recovery, and have found once again that I'm not unique: Many have had like experiences.

From another angle, the recently developed "intervention" technique demonstrates my point. To force alcoholics or addicts to hit bottom and seek help before the disease runs its normal course, families are taught to confront problem users with the consequences of their substance abuse. Trained counselors teach them, one by one, how to describe what their experience of his abuse has been. They don't accuse; they don't blame; they don't batter. They just tell their accounts of his lying, child abuse, financial irresponsibility, emotional instability, arrogance, and grandiosity; of his stinking breath, vomit, physical disintegration, embarrassing behavior, blackouts, car wrecks . . . and all the rest. They learn to speak flatly, factually, and clearly. They let the stories of their experiences speak for themselves; the impact can be overpowering. It can break through even his denial.

Although such interventions don't always work, when they do, they can be powerful and devastating experiences for both the abuser and his family members. Often it's the first time in the living memory of any of them that the truth, the real truth, has been spoken in their family. In sum, then, chemical abusers have a chance of breaking through their denial if their families, their closest communities, can also break through theirs.

Or again, from a still-wider perspective: Until recently, in a couple of societies, alcoholism has been almost nonexistent. Orthodox Judaism and traditional Chinese culture have had no problem historically with alcohol abuse.

Once peoples from those two cultures immigrated to the United States, however, that happy state of affairs began to change for the worse. The immigrants' kids, as they became Americanized, started becoming alcoholic in pretty much the same proportion as the rest of our society. This happened even when Jew married Jew and Chinese married Chinese.

What caused the change? Race and genetics don't explain it. Nor does the use and enjoyment of alcohol; Orthodox Jews and Chinese have used and enjoyed it for centuries. The only thing that's changed for Jews and Chinese in America is that they're in America. No longer self-contained, they're no longer masters of their own values; their wider context has changed.

All of that may sound like nothing more than a point of academic interest—until you translate it into human terms. What if you were the parent of one of those kids? What if your community and religion were so deeply disgusted and shamed by alcoholic behavior that alcoholism just didn't happen—until your daughter or son turned up drunk at a police station, or cold on a morgue slab because of an overdose? What if your values, your faith, your way of life, could no longer speak to your children? How would you feel about this new land you'd come to with such hope? What would you think about American society?

Dealing with a Full Deck

All my life, I've received mixed signals about drinking and drug usage. The spoken, Do-what-I-say message has always been, for the most part, rational and mature: "If you're going to drink, be prudent and careful." The message from adult and societal modeling, the Do-what-I-do message, however, is quite the opposite. In Alaska, where I was raised, one's manhood was often measured by the quantity of alcohol one drank. TV commercials continue to image happiness and success as always including wine or beer. Drunkenness seems to be met more often with laughter and indulgence than disgust and intolerance. It's accepted, winked at, minimized.

On the other hand, the messages my family and society gave me about being mature, grown up, a "Hero" were clear . . . and unambiguous.

From my infancy, the circumstances of my father's death and the spoken messages of my relatives demanded that I was to be strong, "a man." Because I was the oldest (and whether or not anybody told me to), I believed I was somehow supposed to compensate for my compulsive gambler stepfather's terrorizing rages and irresponsibility—to somehow be what he should have been for my mother, brother, and sister. I was supposed to be "big," and "mature," and—above all else—unafraid, because I could rise above my problem through the force of my intelligence. I was supposed to be, I had to be, a Hero—and nothing else.

Those messages were imparted, implanted, and driven home long before my introduction to alcohol. And they carried a weight far beyond the normal: For me, fulfilling those demands was a matter of survival, a matter of life or death.

It made a kind of sense, then: Even my alcoholic denial couldn't win against that kind of programming. When I hit bottom, it was crunch time; and so, unwittingly, I reached for my oldest, deepest, surest survival tools. The Hero *had* to win out over suicide and Skid Road; I had no choice.

So we come to the point: I didn't sit down in my mother's womb, three months before birth, and decide that my fundamental identity and role in life was to be a Hero by age four. Whatever my innate gifts and capabilities, I can say with certainty that *that* program was given to me. I may have cooperated because I had no choice, but, bottom line, in the beginning *I didn't choose it*. Nor would I have continued so steadfastly in my role unless it had been reinforced and demanded by my family and society. It would have been much more fun, all other things being equal, just to be a kid.

As I grew and ventured out into association with other people besides my immediate family, I took with me my training on how to interrelate. I was as I had been taught to be: the little Hero—but rapidly getting bigger. By the time I reached high school, my efforts at being a big, intellectual, unafraid Hero had translated into a nickname from my classmates: the Doctor. Except for actual medical skills, I guess I did fit that vaunted image pretty well, although I hated it and endured it with grudging stoicism . . . yet another trait of a respected and professional Ph.D. Obviously, my con had become so perfected that even I bought it; other people not only believed it, they expected it, for to them *that's who I was*.

The conclusion to be drawn from this is clear. Without others, my denial would not have begun, would not have been embraced, would not have continued, would not have been all-encompassing. At its core, then, a single individual's belief system of denial (like all belief systems) is dependent upon the families and societies that call it into being; it is socially grounded. To a large degree, we—all of us—are what "they" want us to be. It's simply inescapable.

My alcoholic denial was as socially dependent as my ACOA denial. True, *I* discovered that drugs and alcohol worked for me. Yet prior to that personal discovery, there was a doctor who prescribed Valium for me because he and the members of the profession on whose shoulders he stood believed and knew it would work. I found out what alcohol could do for me, but never, even in my most desperate longings for a drink, did I ever distill my own booze or dream up the notion that manliness depended on a man's ability to "hold his liquor."

The denial system that preconditioned my slide into addiction and alcoholism may have come later than my ACOA programming and had about it more ambiguity, but it was just as socially based as the one that sprang from my childhood. And for the most part, it fit that earlier system like hand in glove.

The reverse is true, too. If "they" had not implanted, supported, and demanded from me those denial systems of mine, ninety-nine chances out of a hundred I would not have done as I have done and not have been who I am.

Now, to widen the focus a bit, "they" would not have done as they did unless it had been done to them—and so on, back through and across the generations. We—that is, the human race—have got a problem: Denial and its consequences seem imbedded in our very fiber.

Hanging Together or Hanging Separately

Here, we could get into a pretentious discussion of which came first, the "chicken" of the original alcoholic-addict, or the "egg" of the first family that stumbled onto denial as a way of surviving. Or we could take a pragmatic and practical tack by asking, "Well, what do we *do* about it? How do we *solve* this problem of societal denial?" I'd like to suggest that such a discussion or program aimed at "fixing" what's wrong would, in itself, be only a further exercise in the denial we're trying to understand and eradicate. In fact, by trying to understand it, we'd be trying to control something that, by definition, is uncontrollable.

That last assertion rubs us wrong. It seems to imply that as individuals and as a society we have no choice but to remain victims of our denial systems, slaves to a cruel emotional dilemma: Survival itself demands the defense mechanism of denial, but to live in denial eventually means to die; damned if we do and damned if we don't.

The issue for societies, as for individuals, is survival: We humans, individually and collectively, always do what we believe we must to survive, and denial is first and foremost a survival tool.

An example totally unrelated to chemical dependency may illustrate what I'm getting at. There are enough nuclear weapons in existence today to destroy our world many times over. Likewise, there's never been a weapons system developed that hasn't been used. It seems logical, then, that we should live in the expectation that eventually we'll push the nuclear self-destruct button. Yet if we were all to live in constant, conscious anticipation of what logic says will probably happen, we'd be so paralyzed that our lives would be blocked from happening; that overwhelming consciousness would itself cause us to self-destruct. So we stuff what we know into the back closets of our minds—because we have to—and proceed with our daily rhythms. It's the only way we've got to deal with the stress. We cope with the omnipresent nuclear reality by delegating its management to specialists and choose to trust—because we can't do otherwise—in the basic sanity of those who have the power to push the button. Finally, through laws, treaties, and negotiations, we do what we can to lessen the threat.

In short, we deny the nuclear threat a constant place in our *individual* awareness, yet we balance that denial by realizing the truth of the situation on a *collective* level. We do a constant balancing act, as it were, walking the edge between collective dread and individual hope. We can do little else.

First-year psychology texts describe denial as a useful defense mechanism. We humans have to be able to live in forgetful denial of many things so that we can deal with the tasks at hand. To return to the example, if I'm totally traumatized by a realization of the nuclear threat, my cows probably won't get milked and my books won't bet balanced; I might even be too traumatized to make love. In and of itself, denial's not a bad coping skill to have in one's arsenal. It can at times, in fact, be downright healthy to be in denial.

My individual denial gets into trouble, though, when it's not counterbalanced by a societal awareness. It may, in fact, be healthy for me not to live in fear of the nuclear threat, *but only* if my society, in one way or another, is aware and taking steps to deal with it.

It's that balance between individual denial and societal awareness that's the nub of the problem. It's impossible for any individual practicing chemical dependency or living in codependent and ACOA patterns not to be in denial. That much, I hope, is clear by now. The core of that individual denial is summed up in those trademark claims we discussed earlier: "I can handle my drugs"; "I can handle my alcoholic spouse"; "It really wasn't that bad." Those are precisely the things that we're powerless over, that we cannot handle, that we cannot do. These syndromes own and control us, not we them; so says all the evidence.

A Powerful Contrast

So, if there is going to be a counterbalancing awareness to jolt us out of our individual systems of denial, it must come from the society in which we live. The Orthodox Jewish communities and traditional Chinese society are stunning examples of the power of societal awareness; their collective awareness prevented denial from rooting itself too deeply in any individual. The sense each of those societies had of themselves as a people (and, therefore, what they deemed acceptable in the lifestyles of their individual members) served as an ongoing collective "reality check."

When it comes to chemical dependency, though, I strongly doubt that our modern societies can do for their members what the Jewish and Chinese peoples did for theirs—for several reasons.

First, those two societies—each for its unique reasons—saw themselves to be limited and dependent. Each of them believed themselves to be a "chosen people," but they believed "Someone," "Something Else" had done the choosing. And whether they *remained* "chosen" depended on how well they lived up to the wishes and plans of that "Other." They did not see themselves as masters of their own fate. Thus, built into the very fabric of their self-knowledge was *an acceptance of their powerlessness and dependency in the face of the "Other."*

Our modern societies—capitalist and communist alike—build their sense of themselves on exactly the opposite foundation. Their fundamental presumption is precisely that we human beings can be masters of our own destiny. Everything, *everything,* hinges on that belief of self-sufficiency—because a society constitutionally incapable of seeing itself as limited cannot speak believably to any of its members about powerlessness.

Another way of stating it is that our modern societies—again, both capitalist and communist—put their faith in reason. If there's a problem, we believe we can solve it through the application of elbow grease and intelligence. We're heirs of the Enlightenment. We're prejudiced against seeing any limits to rationality. As a result, we tend to believe that we can think up rational solutions even for emotional problems. (I even presume that I can write something useful, perhaps even profound, about this issue.) But, at heart, chemical abuse, codependency, and ACOA patterns are emotional issues that demand *emotional* resolution, the kind of resolution we children of reason and technology are least prepared even to entertain, much less imagine.

Or, from another angle, once any society gets to be larger than a medium-sized extended family, its members come to know each other, more or less, by their behavior alone. There are just too many people around to be able to get to know them other than superficially—that is, by their behavior. But behavior is only the tip of the human iceberg. We see what many, many people do; we do not see, in most instances, what makes them tick. We enact laws and erect ethical systems to govern behavior. We aim for enough conformity in what people do to keep a modicum of order and, for the most part, we ignore what happens in a person's depths that causes that behavior. Consequently, on a societal level, we almost have to miss the point made earlier: that ". . . drinking is not the point of alcoholism." We have to focus on the drinking and using, the battering and abusive *behavior,* and thus collectively stay unaware of the belief structure of denial that's the real problem. As a society, we don't have the capacity to do otherwise.

In short, our modern societies—at least, as we know them—cannot remain true to themselves without being in denial about the power and intractability of these chemical-abuse issues.

We Have Not Yet Begun to Fight!

It would be unconstitutional (pun intended) to consider ourselves powerless in the face of mere chemicals. If that assertion is anywhere near accurate, its consequences are devastating. A society that is itself in denial can't serve as a collective "reality check" on the denial of its individual members. That means that the most we can expect of a society is that it will be codependent about its alcoholic and addicted citizens—scolding them, punishing them, jailing them—anything but offering them healing and genuine change.

A story about Tom Wojtowick, one of my professional partners, may make all this more concrete. Also a former priest, Tom has been in recovery six years longer than I. A feisty, extroverted character, he can be bluntly tough-minded—at times to the point of near-obnoxiousness. He presumes the worst—namely, that chemical dependents will behave in chemically dependent ways, that codependents will be codependent, and that ACOAs will "ACOA." If an alcoholic disappears from AA meetings, he remarks (loudly), "Guess he's out drinking again." If a codependent starts missing her Al-Anon meetings, it's "She's found somebody new to obsess about." And if ACOAs get huffy and indignant as they're confronted with the emptiness of their lives, he asks with infuriating calmness, "Image got you again?"

In short, Tom "calls bullshit." By doing so, he lives out the tradition of Twelve Step realism—a tradition of pessimism if you wish, but one that those of us who deal with this stuff on a daily basis prefer to call "realistic." If Tom, other hard-core Twelve-Steppers, and chemical-dependency professionals didn't call bullshit, our programs of recovery would all too soon degenerate into communal bitch sessions—conglomerations of embittered, burned-out human husks trading brags about the "good old days."

As a society, we need to be as realistic, as tough-minded as Tom is about alcoholics, codependents, and ACOAs. We need to accept that the world will *never* be perfect (the way we want it to be, the way we wish it were). But we have not.

In effect, what has come to be is a collective denial system that reinforces our individual denial. We are allowed (or, better, *forced*) to be in denial of our denial. As a society, we know the threat of nuclear cataclysm even if, as individuals, we deny it. But when it comes to mind-altering chemicals and their effects, on both levels, societal and individual, we are in denial about the power of the threat. Mushroom clouds are hard to miss—not so another drink or pill taken on the sly. Powerless over alcohol and other chemicals, "We, the People" not only *can* deny, we *must.*

Tom can be disconcerting. He's blunt and often obnoxiously realistic. To survive and thrive in a profession too easily inundated with the insanity of chemical dependency and its wreckage, he's deliberately formed a set of expectations many find uncomfortable. Upon reflection, Tom's pessimistic presumptions, his realism, make all the sense in the world—no matter how much the rest of us squirm at his toughness. What's fascinating, though, is how we do squirm and get irritated with him for his "lack of tact."

A couple of stories can put some more flesh on these ideas. In 1969 and 1970, I was on the boards of directors of two organizations in Bellevue, Washington: Heads Up, a drop-in center for drug-affected youth, and the Eastside Alcoholism Information and Referral Center. In 1970, 1971, and 1972, while on the faculty of a seminary in Baltimore, Maryland, I helped set up and sponsor a hotline run by the seminarians for people with drug problems. I have accolades and testimony that I did effective work for all three of those projects.

Today, though, those accomplishments and accolades tell me nothing more than that I was a superb con. Those projects with which I was involved did good things for people. Nonetheless, they were just more building blocks for my most fundamental alcoholic denial system: If my life could work for everyone else (never mind what it did not do for me), I was not a junkie and a drunk; I could (and did) drink and use.

On top of and as a foundation to my individual denial system, though, there was something else at work. Because of the positions I held (parish priest and faculty member) and because of the nature of the work I was doing (helping people with drug problems), my communities could not and would not see (any more than I could) my steadily progressing chemical dependency and the denial system on which it was based. They focused, as communities must, on my behavior. I was *doing* what they wanted me to do, what they were proud of me for doing. Therefore, it was unthinkable that I could *be* an alcoholic/addict living in denial. It was a genuine vicious circle: They believed me because I was doing what they wanted me to do; they had to believe what they saw; and I believed them, for (like everyone else) I define myself by bouncing against others. A mutual con was going on, focused on my public behavior, in denial of my private truth, designed with exquisite precision to continue the denial. It was Alice-in-Wonderland time—my life worked for everyone else, but not for me.

Alva was the first to deflate the fantasy for me, the first person to take dead-eye aim on my denial and my communities' illusions about me. The first time we talked, he asked me to tell him my story. I did, and, after he stopped laughing, he stared at me with those bulging eyes of his and said, "So, you're a lying, cheating drunk with no self-respect—a failure." In high dudgeon and deeply wounded self-righteousness, I pulled myself up straight to say, "I am *not!*" He just laughed again and, in spite of myself, I started to chuckle, too.

Without a doubt, my family and friends, the members of the various groupings to which I had belonged over the years, would have been even more vigorous than I in my defense—the truth is no more congenial to the chemical dependent's codependents than it is to him.

Those who work with codependents and ACOAs face that solid phalanx of social denial daily. Again and again, I meet people like the mother with ulcers, colitis, asthma, and stress-aggravated heart disease. She pleads with me to see that it's her daughter (recently sentenced to a four-hundred-dollar fine and three sessions of Alcohol Information School for a DWI [Driving While Intoxicated]) who's really got "the problem." The mother gets indignant when I gently try to insinuate that she start an Al-Anon program and take a vacation because her physical health problems are a far more important (and life-threatening) issue than her daughter's first manifestation of problem drinking. After all, she believes *what she has been taught*—that the measure of a mother's worth is her willingness to sacrifice her life for her children. It doesn't even occur to her that it's impossible, genuinely impossible, for one person to take care of another unless she's first taking care of herself. Such is the power of our social denial and romantic stereotyping.

Again, after I've heard the story about another ACOA's forty-six-year-old husband taking up with an eighteen-year-old girl, the ACOA stares at me with angry bewilderment because I'm reluctant to endorse her raging desire to ". . . get a gun and blow the bastard and his floozy away." That I'd suggest that her husband is *not* her problem, and that her desperately dependent, self-abusing, clinging-vine enmeshment with him is—that's just too much. She loves the same way her mother and her mother's mother loved their men. She's been the kind of wife she's *supposed* to be—and that's the point.

Any counselor could multiply the examples ad infinitum. The conclusions would still be the same. Social denial about chemical dependency and the human wreckage it leaves in its wake—the lives and generations molded into codependent and ACOA patterns—is all-pervasive. More than simply pervasive, it fits hand in glove with the underlying presumptions and values of society as we know it.

Seeing the Forest for the Trees

I think it's as difficult for us to get a perspective on this value system of denial as it is for a fish to get a perspective on water. Fish are either in water and alive or out of it and dead. We are either "in" this value system and thus identify with the grounding beliefs of our society or "out" of it and cut off from the roots that give us a sense of belonging and connection with the flow of life around us.

For these reasons, I have strong reservations about all the social/ legal programs our governments and institutions are implementing these days. One of my counselors in treatment told me that she thought that denial had a "smell" to it—an odor, once you became sensitized to it, you could sniff out ten miles away up wind. I "smell" denial in all these "wars on drugs," not in the intentions or goodwill of the people who are trying to do something, but rather in their expectations. The rhetoric of politicians, community activists, and treatment centers claims again and again that we can "win." (I suppose that's the language leaders must use to persuade people to cough up the bucks needed for a "crusade." I'll even concede that most of the people who use that kind of language believe what they're saying.) But, at the risk of being a wet blanket, I wish to say that it is precisely our expectation of "winning," our trust in intelligent legislation, intensified educational programs, toughened laws, and hard work that will doom our efforts. All of those efforts and solutions are from the head; they're rational. The problems, however, are chemical and emotional; even more deeply, they root themselves at the level of value and belief. Those dimensions of the human self seldom modify themselves before law or rationality.

An Anticipated "I Told You So!"

So, then, am I pessimistic? Yes and no—emphatically.

Yes, I'm damned pessimistic if you expect me to have any hope for social programs and "wars on drugs." In Britain and Sweden, legalization has not worked; in the United States, Prohibition was a flop. In spite of Cabinet-level drug czars, Latin American invasions, and military interdictions, I expect more of the same in the nineties.

As a race—when it comes to mood-altering drugs—the only iron-clad guarantee we have about our efforts to fix or eradicate or even modify the problem is Murphy's Law. Sorry, folks, but this one *reason can't win.*

But, no, I'm *not* pessimistic, precisely because I know, in my gut, that reason and technology can't win. I hope we try and try and try. I hope we pour billions into the fight. I hope we raise the national consciousness about the drug problem; and then raise it again. I hope we mobilize the way we did in World War II. The more energy we focus on the issue, the better.

Because the more money, effort, and energy we put into this crusade, the greater the chance that we'll soon be brought to our knees—not in a religious sense but like a boxer whose chin has just met a KO punch. We'll not only lose, *we'll know that we've lost.* This one may—just may—bring us to surrender. It may be the one issue that makes us let go of our faith in our reason and, instead, begin to trust our humanity.

You see, I'm an alcoholic, but I'm not practicing my alcoholism anymore; I'm a codependent, but I'm codepending less and less every day; I'm an ACOA, but today I know—not understand but know—my survival role has next to nothing to do with my life. Those are the facts of my life, and the lives of all in recovery.

Yet those facts are irrational; they don't make sense given the power of chemical dependency, codependency, and ACOA dysfunctions. Recovery simply shouldn't happen; it's simply not reasonable. Nonetheless, it does.

The only explanation I can give you for why it does is a paradox: When I finally surrendered to being addicted and alcoholic, I no longer had to be victimized by my drinking and using. When I surrendered to being dependent, I became free.

You see, those Jewish and Chinese communities knew the secret. They knew they were dependent—however "chosen" they may have been. All we need to do to win our "war on drugs" is to lose our "war on drugs"—and know it.

Chapter 7

Suicide—of the Slow-Motion Kind

The Logical Conclusion
The Ultimate Double Bind
Is Hope a Hype?

People trapped in grim situations often defend their sanity by developing a gallows humor. In that vein, one of the most-repeated themes I hear at Twelve-Step meetings is how we got so sick and made such failures of ourselves that we couldn't even carry through on the one action that would declare to the world how fed up we were with our lives—we flunked suicide. Some real-life examples: "I got ready to jump, but was too drunk to find the cliff"; "I pulled the trigger only to discover I hadn't loaded the gun"; and "I washed down the pills with booze and went into blackout, only to wake up three hours later in the ER because I'd called nine-one-one while I was blacked out."

Doing suicide successfully—and this is from the vantage point of one who couldn't—takes determination and planning. It takes work and coordination. It takes drive.

It's a great blow to realize that you no longer have the self-possession, the determination, the clarity of purpose, to even take your own life.

I've one AA "sponsee" who decided to end it all by jumping off of the Aurora Bridge in Seattle. It's probably a three-hundred-foot drop to the Ship Canal below, so he felt fairly certain he'd be able to do an adequate job. He chose to make his leap at about 3:00 A.M.; that way, there'd be little chance of somebody seeing him and trying to interfere. He climbed up and out on the railing, then jumped. It should have worked—but he'd forgotten two things. He's fairly small, solid but small, and he'd picked a night when the wind was blowing with fifty-knot gusts. Just as he jumped, the wind whooshed, and he landed not in the canal but on his rump, sitting in the middle of the bridge's roadway. In disgust, he decided to check into a local treatment program. When he told me about it the next day, I truly didn't know whether to laugh or cry. And, yes, despite his careful plans, there *was* a witness to corroborate his story.

Suicide: Healthy and Unhealthy

At this point, I want to make clear that suicidal feelings and actions are different for us addictive dependents than for relatively healthy people. For the healthy person, the impulse to suicide is extraordinary. Even in the healthiest of lives, "shit happens" occasionally— the tragic death of a child, the shattering of a career, the onslaught of a terminal disease, war, etc. When bowled over by such events, I suppose it's only human to think of suicide—and perhaps even to do it—although such aberrant bouts of despair usually resolve themselves with a good cry, short-term therapy, or the support and solace of loved ones.

But being chemically dependent, codependent, or ACOA are not once-or-twice-in-a-lifetime events. They are habitual lifestyles of denial, as we've discovered. And for us, therefore, whose whole lives are about the opposite of everything being true, suicide is a different story—it's our constant and *ordinary* companion.

Suicide's the one human action that's absolutely foolproof—when it works. It grabs other people's attention like nothing else. I've one client whose mother committed suicide. He's now married to an extremely manipulative alcoholic whose trump card in any argument is the threat to do herself in. He's yet to be able to stand up to her. The memories of Momma's death are still too raw, although it happened over twenty-seven years ago.

But for us addictive dependents, suicide's even more than the perfect attention-getting device; it's also the perfect guilt trip. Precisely because we're in denial of our dependencies, our internal ethic demands we be ashamed when we cry out for that attention. So, since a suicide (by definition) can't be around to enjoy the fruits of his labors, his self-destruction both gets him what he wants and bestows upon him the appropriate punishment for wanting it. It's ironic in a macabre way: "The punishment fits the crime. . . ."

It's no exaggeration to say that our lifestyle of denial finds its ultimate meaning in suicide. Take a look at it. In each of these syndromes, the goal of the lifestyle is always shutdown. Addictive abuse of any drug—even speed or cocaine—ultimately leads to such distortion and depression that one's real emotional life is suppressed and obliterated. What chemical dependents do to themselves pharmacologically, codependents achieve through depression and compulsive loss of themselves in the lives of their beloved. And ACOAs, to survive their family snake pits, repress and cancel out their feeling lives to produce carefully crafted images that are all front and no substance—images so powerful, so convincing, that they con even their inventors.

Life, first and foremost, occurs in the heart, not the head. (That's the reason computers, no matter how sophisticated, will never qualify as life-forms.) We habitually spend our lives depressing, anesthetizing—denying—our hearts: in short, doing emotional self-destruction on a daily basis. Day in and day out, we've gazed into ourselves and—sometimes clearly, sometimes dimly—seen at our center . . . nothing. That ongoing intimation, that perception of unrelieved nothingness, explains why suicide is the logical outcome, the normal and ordinary goal of our habitual denial.

Nothing

Frankly, it's damned difficult to speak of nothingness, to explore the empty. Confronted with that task, our language, intelligence, and imaginations find themselves inadequate and immobilized, but let's take a stab at it anyway.

When I was about three years sober, I woke up around three or three-thirty one morning, curled up fetus-like, shaking with terror. It came in waves, starting in my feet, rolling up through my body, and out through the top of my head. Off and on throughout the years, I'd woken up like that. Sometimes because of a nightmare, sometimes not, I'd sit bolt upright in bed vibrating with that terror, expecting my heart to beat out of my chest. Up to the night in question, I'd deal with it by turning on the lights and forcing myself to read or watch TV. Slowly, I'd push "it" back down, somehow relocking the chains of willpower that allowed me to live most of the time unmoved by such disconcerting emotions.

This night, though, it wouldn't be stopped. In my panic, all I could think of was to call Andy, my closest AA friend. He usually sleeps like the dead, but for once he heard the phone and answered. I can't remember what I said or how I worked through it all, but I do remember that he did a very wise, very "program" thing. He didn't tell me not to be afraid; he didn't pooh-pooh what was happening; he didn't tell me to buck up and be strong. He simply "walked with me," over the telephone, for close to an hour. He felt my terror, respected it, let it happen. In the end, honored, I quieted and went back to bed.

To this day, I don't have a complete reading of what that attack of terror was all about, yet I have some sense of its meaning. More than anything else, I'm sure, it was about my journey into and through nothingness. I'd come to that point in my healing where "none of it" worked anymore. My alcoholic denial was shattered, my code-pendent and ACOA patterns stood revealed as empty—and I felt as though there were nothing left. That was the most terrifying thing about my terror: I wasn't afraid of anything specific; there was no object to the feeling; I was just . . . terrified. It was overwhelming; it was empty; and I felt like I was going to die.

Denying Our Need to Belong

In the 1920s, Adler pointed out that panic attacks result directly from the fear of no longer belonging.[1] When all our illusions and imagined identities shatter, we feel as never before that we no longer belong. We realize starkly that our lifestyles were devised *only* so that we could survive. In our bones, we know we don't survive if we don't belong.

But *belonging* is what dependency of any kind is about. The chemical dependent belongs to his drug of choice: codependents codepend to belong to their beloved; and ACOAs "ACOA" through the use of their survival roles in order to belong to a family always threatening to abandon them.

But that's only the first part of the setup. Our need to belong is only the first part of our story, since our disease has to double back on itself, as it were, to make us be in denial of that need. And that denial once more makes the opposite true. The denial within which we set our dependencies has the purpose of telling us we don't belong—to the world that drives us to drink, to the spouse who abuses our love, to the families who terrorize our childhoods.

So those chemically dependent, codependent, and ACOA states of dependency (surrounded by our lifestyles of denial) bear within their self-contradiction the seeds of their own destruction. The ever-deepening, chemically induced isolation of addiction and alcoholism; the progressive numbing of codependent depression; the inexorable, devastating exhaustion of being an ACOA obeying the dictates of role—all of them have only two possible outcomes if carried to their furthest extremes. They either kill directly or they collapse from within of their own weight.

When they collapse, and we, their believers, hit bottom, what shatters most of all are the identities they've given us—and then we no longer belong. Concretely put: If I accept I *am* an alcoholic, I'm nothing more than a common drunk, no longer a sophisticated drinker but a Skid Road outcast. If I accept I *am* a codependent, I'm

---

[1] Cf. Harold H. Mosak, "Adlerian Psychotherapy," in *Current Psychotherapies,* ed. Raymond J. Corsini (Itasca, IL: T. E. Peacock Publishers, 1984), pp. 56–107.

no longer the world's greatest unrequited lover; I'm a lugubrious, manipulative, self-pitying, lovesick puppy who's very boring to everyone else. If I accept I *am* ACOA, I am no hero; I'm a terrified little child, expecting abandonment, scared to death, and useless to the grown-up world. For people with egos as inflated as ours, given those alternatives, many of us would rather die than switch—and *do* when the truth comes home to roost.

So, for a while after self-realization, it's as if suicide has us surrounded: It's suicidal to live in denial, but it also seems suicidal to shatter our denial. We've arrived at the final and culminating double bind, the last and greatest "damned if you do and damned if you don't" denouement of our Alice-in-Wonderland world of dependency and addiction. If we stay in our denial and progress in our dependency, we will kill ourselves. The suicidal nature of our deaths may camouflage itself behind a car accident or a stress-induced heart attack or any of a myriad other ways. Nonetheless, bottom line, we are the unconscious perpetrators of our own deaths. Yet if we break through the denial by hitting bottom and facing our truth, that process threatens our very belonging. It brings us face-to-face with our emptiness, and has led more than one of us to end it all.

This brings us back to my friend who tried jumping off the Aurora Bridge and the final great irony. By the time most of us see where we've headed, we don't have the resources left to obey the inner logic of it all. We have become such failures that we even *have* to flunk suicide, no matter how intense our longing to end it all.

In a way, though, such a lack of wherewithal seems appropriate and fitting. The universal emotional state of anyone programmed into the later stages of this kind of denial is guilt. Guilt demands punishment—and no punishment fits our "crime" better than having to linger on, borne down by the wreckage of our lives and unable to get it over with.

Thus, I'm convinced that the "brand" of suicide we addictively dependent people usually is practice "slow motion" in nature. From the first moment a user crosses the line into addiction, or a codependent lover loses his self-possession in the life of his beloved, or a child in a chemically abusive family has to choose denial in order to survive, the seeds of self-destruction are sown.

But this kind of suicidal denial is like dry rot. It corrodes slowly from the inside. The stuff is progressive, and its progress—especially in codependents and ACOAs—is imperceptible. It takes years of erosion before all the foundations crumble and we wake up to realize our lives aren't working. In short, the suicidal process of our denial systems moves at the same speed as our lives, for they become one and the same.

The Legacy of Suicide

Suicide then, to repeat, is the ultimate act of anger and rejection. It's the epitome of self-punishment. It's the culmination of despair. It's the loudest possible cry for attention. It's the fulfillment of self-punishing guilt. Among some peoples and classes, it has been the final proof of one's honor and dedication. And I suspect, in some few instances, it has even been a pondered out and peaceful acceptance of the inevitable.

Since by definition, neither you nor I have been there (this is one instance of "close" not really counting) and even those who've undergone "near-death experiences" still have to guess about the final outcome of the act, all we can attest to with certainty is how we experience another's death.

On the basis of that experience, suicide seems the most individual of actions—when you take it at face value. And maybe that face value speaks the truth if we're talking about the occasional suicide of an emotionally healthy person—the man who's dying of a painful and incurable disease and rationally chooses to end his pain, for example.

But, once again, when we get to the suicides of chemical dependents, codependents, and ACOAs, there's more to it than meets the eye. In an extreme sense, we are the offspring and heirs of the contexts from which we sprang. The job of the healthy family and a healthy lifestyle is to set its children free; the unspoken but oh-so-real goal of *our* families and lifestyles was to keep us chained.

For us, suicides—done quickly or acted out in slow motion—beget suicides. If a parent does it, the odds increase dramatically that one or several of the children will choose it, too. It's as if suicidal parents make the possibility of suicide real for the children—in a strange way, give their children permission to kill themselves.

I'd sketch the inner logic of it this way: Since most of the time suicide is an act of rage against one's family, society, and world, those close to a suicide will feel the power of his anger, and will probably blame themselves, at least for a while, for his death. That's even truer if we are codependent or ACOA—which is almost inevitably the case in these situations.

The guiltier I feel, however, the angrier in turn I'm going to be at the one who laid the guilt on me by killing himself. On top of that, if I'm not only feeling guilty but am an addict/alcoholic/codependent/ACOA, most likely I'll turn that anger inward against myself. A classic question people who work on suicide hotlines ask those who call them is, "Who do you really want to kill?" For that's the result of such anger turned inward: Too often, in a strangely perverted kind of revenge, the suicide gets even with the one who's inflicted guilt upon him by taking his own life. From the outside, that seems to be the logic of the process. Guilt, after all, is living out—or in this case, dying out—somebody else's anger.

We may have loved our parents; we may have hated them; but, inevitably, they were our role models. Sometimes, their message was refracted through intervening generations, but like waves in the Southern Ocean, it rolls on unchecked to us. And where there was the angry devastation of their slow-motion suicides, there will be the slow-motion guilt and revengeful self-destruction of our own. These belief systems of denial and their consequences, by and large, are no accident.

The Wider View

I hope at this point it becomes clear why I believe the previous chapter on the "social dimensions of denial" is so important. We're now talking generations of families; we're talking society. We're not speaking about isolated individuals taking their own lives, alone and cut off from everybody else. Rather, we're talking about an interlocking, intensifying, growing social pattern. If this is a disease, then it's a social disease whose presenting claim is "We're (I'm) not sick."

Social scientists, philosophers, pundits, and preachers who debate issues like society's fate, the problem of evil, and the rise and fall of cultures may find some earthshaking message in that. There's part of me—maybe the preacher part, maybe the alcoholically grandiose part—that would love to pull up a soapbox and do the same. I think, however, that would only cloud the facts. Chemical dependency and suicide are not newcomers to the human scene. If the people who study these things are correct, societies and civilizations come and go, yet the percentage of people chemically addicted remains constant in all of them. Likewise, people have been committing suicide throughout human history. And I doubt that anyone could prove that either fact has had much impact on the ultimate outcome of anything.

The one thing I do know is that an awful lot of people are going through a very painful and prolonged way of dying. When we look from the inside at the "whys" and "wherefores" of it all, it does make a morbid kind of sense; it has a peculiar logic of its own. But from the outside, it seems a horrible waste—a kind of human variant of the lemmings' death march to the sea. Most of all, it hurts. I believe the story of our "Death March" in slow motion, told without moralizing or interpretation—the story alone, unvarnished and unglossed—is the one thing that can connect us to the pain of it all. And maybe when we connect to that pain, we'll be able to find in ourselves the ability to grieve, and thus the motivation to change.

So here, as in Chapter 6, my goal is to tell the story as accurately and starkly as I can. And if you find the story to be gloomy and despairing—fatalistic, even—then I've achieved my goal, for we'll have got to the emotional truth.

Suicidal Choice: A Note About Storytelling

Ancient storytellers and modern novelists have always know a truth about stories. They need to be told—honestly, simply, straightforwardly. In their very telling, if the stories are true, something happens. Hearts are touched, and when hearts are touched, people change. That's the power, for example, of a well-made TV documentary.

I believe the same sort of change can happen even with a story as ugly as the one I've been relating. The facts, unvarnished, uninterpreted, and "unmoralized," are enough. Whenever I view my life and behavior through the lens of what I "should" do, I stay defensive and unchanged. I stay frozen because I feel judged.

Only when I realized I could take my own life did I stumble onto the insight existential psychologists had been aware of for almost fifty years: If I can choose to end my life, I can also choose to live it—no matter how I'd been programmed. If I've learned how to die, I can also learn how to live.

Thus, the strangest twist (for me) to the opposite of everything being true has been the discovery of freedom in the face of my suicidal programming. It has been a freedom that came *only* when I was able to tell myself and my personal world my story, truthfully, acceptingly, without judgment. I don't have a completely rational explanation why such a turnabout should occur, but I do know that when everything finally hung together, I felt relaxed, at peace, and even refreshed. The "Committee" in my head finally shut up, and I was able both to cry and to laugh, to grieve and to celebrate.

We people of denial are creatures of extremes, and there's nothing more extreme than suicide. So maybe we're only fulfilling the deepest dictates of our genes and programming and disease when we live out our patterns of slow-motion self-destruction. Whatever, my own journey has taught me that all the reasons, all the "shoulds" and "oughts" my world gives me to live, can retard my personal "Death March" just about as effectively as a child's sand castle can hold back the sea. If anything, paradoxically, those "reasons" and "shoulds" and "oughts" actually fueled the March. But the story, laid bare in its stark truth without judgment—that alone changed everything and freed me: I could at last choose life for myself and not for "them."

Chapter 8

The World Turned Upside Down

Conclusion to Part One

Time to take a break—catch our breath. We've slogged our way through some pretty heavy material in the last several chapters, and now it's time to rest awhile and take stock.

If I were you, I think I'd be almost overwhelmed right now, and maybe even angry at me. We've just picked our way through the middle of the insidious, baffling world of dependency and denial. To see it in its stark ugliness has to be overwhelming. Besides, I promised you some humor and hope—and there's been precious little of either for quite a while. So, as I said, I'd expect you to be angry, maybe even to feel like I've suckered you with those promises of "Good News."

There's a method to my madness. Humor and hope are peculiar emotions. We can only recognize and savor them fully against backdrops of their opposites. If pompous hypocrites routinely did ten pratfalls a day on banana peels, pratfalls would lose their punch. And as Chesterton once said, ". . . hope can only be hope when everything is hopeless."[1] So, I've been busy with the backdrop, deliberately painting it as black as possible.

[1] Chesterton, op. cit., p. 93.

That's not really been too hard. If anything, this shadow land of addictive dependency and denial is worse than any description I could dream up. Once you've been there with the blinders off, there's not much in the way of human misery, malfunction, and inhumanity that's surprising. Hitler and Stalin, after all, were spawned from families like those we've been describing, and in our country, the genocidal eradication of Native Americans was wreaked far more by alcohol than bullets. The story *is* horrifying.

So where's the hope? The rule of thumb I heard at an AA meeting may begin to open the window: ". . . the more extraordinary the story, the more ordinary the drunk [include, as well, the codependent and the ACOA]." We've been exploring a story so extraordinary in its emptiness and despair that it's easy to miss the ordinary, common, everyday thread of hope running right through its core. The human spirit is limitlessly adaptable when faced with the need to survive; and the story we've been telling is one exposition of that very adaptability. I believed I'd die if I didn't drink and use, so I drank. I believed I'd die without my beloved, so I gave possession of my very life to my love. I believed I'd die if my image were ever to fail, so I became my role. I adapted and did what I had to do to survive according to my lights. I would and did do anything to survive, and so, I bet, would you.

That's the point to this black, black backdrop: If we can see—in spite of what we believed in the past—that our very survival *today* demands we adapt by changing and letting go of those beliefs that have run our lives, I'm willing to bet we've got a real chance to heal—no matter the odds against us. The very part of us that got us and kept us in this pickle in the first place—our need to survive— is the very thing, the only thing, that can get us out of it. If we're scared to death we'll "go to any lengths," even the risk of death, in order to live. So, if you're scared by the story, scared to death even (in your gut and not just your head)—it's worked. For unlike your head, your gut can't lie—at least, I've discovered mine can't. Guts tell the truth, and "the truth shall make [us] free," even if that truth's about blackness and death.

Alva's fond of calling chemical dependency a "life skill." He tells an earthy little parable about ". . . the teenage kid at his first high school dance who's too scared to ask any of the girls out on the floor to boogie. His best buddy pulls him into the men's room, gives him a swig and a toke—and suddenly our hero can walk up to anyone. If she says, 'No, you're too skinny, and you've probably got pimples on your butt,' he can stare her in the eye and say, 'Fuck you very much'—then swagger off to find somebody else who's prettier anyway." Chemicals work, just like the codependent's caring and the ACOA's role work.

That is, they work until they don't. They're "life skills" or (better in our context) "survival skills" that eventually fail. They turn on us. Invariably, when they do, when the anesthesia hurts more than the pain it's anesthetizing, we find we're hooked. We can't dance without the drugs. We can't mix without the drinks. We can't live without our loves. The tools we took up to control our lives have somehow turned the tables. They're in the saddle now and ride us, and ride us, and ride us, it seems, to the very death.

So we fight, and the more we fight them, the stronger those "tools" become, the more power we give them. The more we try to reassert control, the more they win.

People who know the woods and the wilds say that if you fall into white-water rapids or quicksand, the quickest way to go under and die is to fight. They say you can only survive if you relax and let yourself float, surrender to the water or sand and trust them, let them have the control—for they will anyway.

That's the great, huge, practical joke of it all. *Our enemy's the enemy only if we make it so.* That's true even of death itself. The big problem is not that we're going to die. Everyone does that. For us for whom the opposite of everything is true, the problem is that we're probably going to die like *that:* isolated, toxic, paranoid, bitter, exhausted, confused, empty, fighting, and before our time. That's the horror.

So, healing, then, is about relaxing and reconnecting and learning how to float. It's about surrendering the fight, and turning instead to trust. It's about telling the truth and then becoming able to laugh and cry.

Aristotle, long ago, said there are three things that move us humans: "beauty, truth, and goodness." He said as well that we're "social animals." Augustine had a beautiful Latin phrase, "*cor ad cor loquiam*," "heart speaking unto heart." Healing happens when my heart can speak to your heart and not just your head, when we can begin to tell the truth together and discover life's good beauty.

That's what "*The Good News*" is about.

Part Two

"The Good News"

Chapter 9

Which Way Is Up?

What Goes Back into the Hole?

As we discussed in Chapter 7, the realization and acceptance that I was alcoholic, codependent, and ACOA was not—of itself—delightful or peace-giving. Hitting bottom brought me face-to-face with my black hole, and I find the experiences of my clients parallel my own. Again and again, once their denial shatters and they realize their emotional nakedness, they look at me or the members of their support groups and demand, "*Now* what? I've come apart at the seams. How do I get put back together?"

Living in our dependencies and denial may not have been fun, but at least it was fairly easy, since it was predictable. In the same sense, the dysfunction we've discussed in "The Bad News" has been "easy," since the patterns are all so predictable.

"Alcoholic people do alcoholic things." So do addicts, codependents, and ACOAs. Despite the variety of our personalities and circumstances, the plot lines of our dysfunction and denial remain the same. They have a coherent dynamic and consistent logic—even, as that treatment counselor of mine said, an unmistakable "smell." Most of all, it's what we're used to.

Recovery and healing change everything; they introduce a wild card into the game—freedom. If addiction, dependency, and denial are about slavery, then healing must be about freedom. And freedom is about choices, options, surprises, and unpredictability and transcendence. Like art, there's no single way to go about healing, because it is about the unshackling of creativity; its possibilities are as numerous as the individuals who embark on the journey.

A Word to the Wise

I have some personal concerns in approaching this part of my book. First, I've found a way of recovery that (at least until today) works for me. I'm quite susceptible to that very human process I outlined earlier: how an approach to doing something moves from "*a* way" into being "*the* way." Thus, I'm acutely conscious as I begin this section that I may sound like a "true believer."

On top of that, I tend to preach (naturally enough), and I tend to judge quite critically any approaches that differ from the one I'm committed to. Since I'm alive today, I have no apologies for what I believe in.

But I wouldn't be surprised if you find yourself resisting—strongly, perhaps—what I've got to say in the second half of this book. In fact, I would encourage you to resist it, fight it, chew at it. Freud is supposed to have commented to the effect that 90 percent of therapy consists of identifying one's resistance and finding out what it's about.

That said, in "The Good News" we'll explore the process of recovery, looking again in turn at chemical dependents, codependents, and ACOAs. I want to investigate with you how and why such changes happen, what their dynamics are, and what their results are. Because it's so irrational that healing would occur, I presume I'll be no more able than anyone else to offer an unassailable explanation for this process. These days, however, presuming inadequacy is strangely comforting: It may mean I'm breaking free from my self-imposed demand for omniscience.

If there's truth in what I have to say, it's a practical truth, not some unchangeable revelation from on high. When it comes to recovery, I'm interested in results: If what I offer *works,* if it helps you get better, then it's as true as it need be. If and when more effective approaches come along, then they'll be truer in the sense I'm using, and it would behoove all of us to fiercely grab hold of them.

The Practicality of Beliefs

So, let's proceed. The world of addictive dependency we've been exploring is many things. It's a "place" of chemical enslavement, compulsive behavior, devastating programming, distorting confusion, despair, and slow-motion suicide. Above all else, though, it is a netherworld founded upon and determined by a belief system of denial. As we've seen in earlier chapters, that belief system has individual and social dimensions; its purpose is survival; its consequence is death.

And so, to begin the process of healing, we must discover some "something" that can replace (override, supplant) our existing belief system of despair and denial. Arguments and logic cannot overthrow systems of belief and value. Education, by itself, cannot reverse their flow. What is needed is "something" that will (almost literally) *move our hearts.*

Recall Aristotle's reflection that "beauty, truth, and goodness"— and they alone in the long run—will move human hearts. What is needed is a more *attractive,* compelling belief system. The "disease" part of our addiction may require the services of an internist or psychiatrist. But doctors don't heal dependency. No, this belief system can only be "cured" if it is replaced by another belief system.

In the first chapter of "The Bad News," I described belief systems as habits, grooved channels that guided the rivers of our lives. Now, we have to consider implanting and nurturing habits of *life* in the place of habits of *death.* We will be searching for "counter-habits" whose course might guide us to choose self-creation instead of self-extinction.

But there are belief systems and then there are belief systems. Religions are belief systems. The patriotism one has for a country is a belief system. Military esprit de corps is a belief system. To call oneself a Hoosier or a Republican or a vegetarian is to profess belief. To be a fan of the Seattle Seahawks instead of the Chicago Bears is an act of belief (and, in some years, an act of credulity).

I enjoy the challenge of studying belief systems. They're absolutely basic to purposeful human living, yet they so permeate our lives that it's easy to miss them. Like a faithful dog, they're always there; like eyeglass lenses, they're right in front of our eyes, but most often we're oblivious to them. We depend on them to structure our lives, and so trust them to be "right" that we're astonished when we encounter somebody whose values differ from ours.

Our interest is not anthropological or sociological, but practical, because beliefs are practical. They're about action; they guide us in how to go about the jobs of living; they're the underlying channels of our conscious lives and, as such, are foundational to our doing and thinking. They're the stuff of all our unspoken "shoulds" and "oughts."[1]

Belief systems fulfill two of the most basic human needs: They give us a sense of belonging and a sense of identity. I dare you, for example, to belong as an American without, at some level, to some degree, believing in American values. Even our identities as women or men are defined as much by the ways we believe men and women "should" be as they are by our respective anatomies. Consequently, belief systems are the source of meaning, not so much in an intellectual sense but in a psychological way—the source of identity.

How Can We Know We're "Right"?

Is there any criterion we can use to judge which set of beliefs might steer us toward recovery and which won't? I think there is. It's the

---

[1] If I'm a carpenter, for example, I "should" approach my woodworking in such-and-such a way to do it successfully. It would be the same if I want to be a successful scientist, parent, spouse, citizen, cook, friend, curmudgeon, salesperson, or teammate. There are ways to do it and ways to screw it up—and the odds are that if I don't follow the guidance and wisdom offered by a tested set of values and beliefs, I'll do the latter.

same criterion an alcoholic uses to judge the effectiveness of his use of booze and denial—*whether it works*. An alcoholic will practice his disease—just like addicts, codependents, and ACOAs—as long as it continues to work. To paraphrase Freud, this denial lifestyle works for us as long as it helps us avoid pain and provides an illusion of pleasure. In fact, a good working description of "bottom" is that it's the "moment" we realize our lives no longer work, but hurt; the "moment" when our belief is shattered; the "moment" we realize that the anesthesia hurts more than the pain it was anesthetizing.

My assertion—my conviction—is that for lasting sobriety, the lifestyle and belief system of chemically dependent denial must be shattered and replaced. Something like what happens to participants in the AA Program must come about if sobriety is to come about.

The Distinction Between Healing and Programs

Thus, I intend to use AA and the other Twelve-Step programs as models (clear and strong examples, if you wish) of the underlying process of healing. (Much as I endorse AA, there were people who got sober before the founding of the Program.[2] There are people today who do it without employing the Program. There's even the occasional case of what can only be called "spontaneous remission."[3] The point here is not to convert you to the Twelve-Step programs, but rather to investigate the remarkable healing results that have occurred for people who were willing to "bet their lives" on exploring what these programs have to offer.)

To emphasize: Being a member of Twelve-Step programs is my personal preference. It's what works for me, but I've no desire to push it down anyone else's throat. *Really!* What I *am* interested in is the dynamic underlying the shattering and replacement of denial.

[2]Nan Roberts, *Getting Better* (New York: William Morrow, 1988), pp 43–46.
[3]Whitfield, op. cit. p. 5.

Let me be clear about what I do not mean by "healing." I do not see the removal of something—even chemicals—from a person's life as anything more than a negative action—an absolutely necessary action, perhaps, but negative nonetheless. For example, an alcoholic may get dry by stopping drinking, but getting *dry* is not getting *sober*. In my opinion, getting sober entails the implanting and development of a new lifestyle to supplant and replace the lifestyle of denial. It means constructing a new belief system grounded above all else in something completely different . . . honesty.

Likewise for codependent and ACOA belief systems. It's not enough "just" to let go of the beloved to whom one is addicted or abandon the all-consuming image role one has played. Codependents and ACOAs must undergo transformations of belief and lifestyle, too. If not, like dry alkies or nonusing junkies, they will be living out nothing more than emotional "dry drunks." The only thing that will have changed is that their lives will now have "holes" that once were filled. People on dry drunks are the pits to work with. Their emotional hallmarks are usually depression and anger; their intellectual spoor is stubborn confusion. As a general rule, I'd rather deal with practicing dependents than dry drunks. They're much more fun and nowhere near so angrily rigid.

What I do mean by healing is getting to the truth of our lives and telling it (living it) honestly. By no means do I live out that kind of honesty with any perfection. But to the extent that I do, I experience a fascinating change. When I was drinking or doing a full-fledged job of practicing my codependency and ACOA roles, I told myself—by doing so—that I was different, that I didn't belong.

Recovery has given me quite a comeuppance, though, because the most egodeflating realization I've yet bumped into is that I was anything but different. I was boringly, tiresomely, predictably, *exactly* the same as any other ACOA, codependent, or drunk. I'd been doing and being exactly what *any* such person would do or be. I was a conformist despite all my posturing. I may have felt completely cut off, alone, and different, but the truth was, I was a most ordinary addictive dependent—a self-deluding clone.

The freedom of recovery has given me my uniqueness, my specialness as an individual. I'm not always sure what to do with that uniqueness, or even always comfortable with it, but I can't deny that today my life has become an adventure—for the first time.

Most surprisingly of all, I'm discovering that, in my uniqueness—maybe even because of it—I'm not alone. I belong, and (God forbid!) I enjoy it. By becoming an "AA clone," I'm finally free to find my personal specialness.

Jung termed the process of growing into a healthy, adult maturity as *individuation,* becoming one's own unique person. That, at its root, is what I think recovery's hope is all about—and describes the reach of the following chapters.

Chapter 10

The Heart of Surrender

Chemical Dependency and Coming Home to the Truth

A snide brunette once remarked to me, "Blond isn't just a hair color; it's a way of life." Likewise for chemical dependency: It's not just a disease; it, too, is a way of life. Because of that, I'm amazed any of us heal. Recovery makes no sense: With all the odds against us, because of the tenacity with which our lifestyle grips us, healing should be nothing more than a pipe dream. And it may seem at this point that no matter how hard we try to change the "color" of our lives, the roots will keep growing back . . . it'll never be more than a "dye-job."

Some of us begin this topsy-turvy life they call sobriety more than half a bubble off-center and two bricks short of a load, like the man who made one of Guest House's more delightfully comic grand entrances. About four months into my treatment, I stood in the hall-way one afternoon, looking out the French-doored windows into the drive winding in from the highway. A long, long gray Cadillac limousine with gold-trimmed wire wheels pulled up to the main entrance. A chauffeur, uniformed in navy blue and spit-shined black boots, got out and walked into the office. Minutes later, the treatment center's head counselor accompanied him back out to the limo. The chauffeur opened the passenger door, dipping his head and clicking his heels (I kid you not) as he did so. Out emerged this tall, slim, black-goateed priest in his thirties, attired in a pearlgray, double-breasted suit with a black vest to set off his Roman collar. His right hand, pinky extended, held a tall, fluted, three-quarter-full champagne glass; his left drifted out in front of him elegantly, indolently, as though he were the half hearted conductor of a Viennese waltz. With head counselor and chauffeur *en train*, he glided into the building, through the office, and down the main hall where ten or twelve of us "inmates" had gathered by now for the show. He took the hallway in swooping S-curves, bowing greeting and benediction to each of us as he passed, never spilling a drop as he careened in slow motion from wall to wall. We gave him a standing ovation as he ascended the main stairway to his room.

Others of us begin sobriety so cocooned in control, rationalization, and a desperate balancing act that the slightest nudge of spontaneity would flip us out like an overwound clock spring. That was me. I scrambled to prove my intelligence and worth to all comers. I argued theology with my fellow residents in treatment. I gave the counselors gratuitous lectures on their therapeutic technique. I was such a quick study, I took it upon myself to explain the AA Program to people who'd been sober for five years. Never had I been so desperate to prove myself.

Yet whatever our condition, overwrapped or screws loose, we do come to treatment and Program. Sometimes we're court-ordered into it or forced by employers; sometimes we're tricked into it; sometimes it's even voluntary, motivated by pain and a realization that there's no place else to turn. But, once we're there, the fun begins. . . .

At my first meeting, some "old-timers" told me AA was about "experience, strength, and hope." Although the words were gentle, their manner was gruff; they gave me my marching orders: "Go to meetings. Don't drink and use between meetings. Get a sponsor. Work the Steps and follow directions . . . which are: Go to meetings. Don't drink or use between meetings. Get a sponsor . . . etc."

I said, "But—" and they rudely interrupted, "Just do it. We know how not to drink; you don't."

As introductions go, that one lacked tact, but it was at least clean and honest. What really stung was that I knew they spoke the truth: I *didn't* know how not to drink and use. That it should be raspy-voiced former drunks, sitting around in a dingy room gulping generic-brand coffee (out of Styrofoam cups, for God's sake) who were the bearers of that message did not improve its palatability. I mentally rolled my eyes and muttered an exclamation that has since been identified to me as the "Short Form of the Serenity Prayer": "Ahhh, fuck!"

I'm not quite sure how I smelled that evening. Vodkalike, probably—I'm pretty certain that was the last thing I'd had to drink. (This in itself is one of the surer proofs I was on bottom: I'd been so out of control I couldn't even make it to my first AA meeting smelling like my favorite liquors, Scotch or brandy. Vodka?!—I hated vodka!) The night was capped off when my new, self-appointed sponsor (Alva) took me outside for a walk, asked me what my story was, and then laughed when I told him.

Two things made me stay. I didn't want to hurt like that anymore, and John, the man who'd brought me to the meeting, had forewarned me, "You'll hear a lot tonight. Some of it you'll like; some you won't. It's an individual program: Take what you need and leave the rest."

And there was something else . . . these people were laughing! I didn't like them; I didn't particularly want what they said they had. But I *did* want that laughter. In fact, more than once during the intervening years the only reason I've not drunk or used has been the same: fear of losing that laughter.

Pain and laughter seem to be the flip sides of the coin of recovery. I heard somebody at a meeting once say, "I wanted to commit suicide—not to die, but to stop the pain." All of us there nodded; we identified; and then we chuckled in agreement.

My second meeting, I walked in, sat down, looked across the

table, and saw an old drinking buddy from my first parish side by side with one of my former altar boys. They both winked, then grinned, then laughed—and, literally for the first time in my life, I felt as though I'd come home. I blushed. I winked back, I grinned . . . then I laughed, too.

Getting to the Bottom

You can lead a horse to water, but you can't make him drink—especially if he doesn't know he's thirsty. For example, a couple of months ago I was forced to concede that my years had ambushed my eyes. I needed to get glasses—not "just reading glasses" but full-time, all-day-long spectacles. The optometrist was one of those achingly upbeat people who kept a line of patter flowing as he fiddled with various lenses, searching for the best combination to correct my eyesight. Some fuzzed things up even more; others sharpened my focus. But finally he hit on a set of lenses that made the smallest letters on his chart stand out in clear relief.

As my sight cleared, though, my head suddenly felt as if somebody were driving in a spike right behind my eyes. The pain was excruciating. I let out a yelp and begged him to tell me what was going on. He replied that he'd found the optimum focus for my eyes, and my optical muscles were relaxing from the tension they'd been under. That caused the pain. The magnitude of that muscular "letting go" was almost literally mind-blowing.

I thought about how much energy I'd unconsciously used day after day to force my eyes into focus, compensating for my steadily blurring vision. I hadn't had a checkup in over ten years (And yes, I *know* it's my job to tell people to take care of themselves). The doctor told me the degeneration had probably been gradual over the past several years and that the contortions and spasms my eye muscles had to put themselves through had been slow-developing and imperceptible. It was automatic: I hadn't deliberately chosen to abuse my eyes; nonetheless, I had been gradually slipping into an illusion, a fantasy—which I believed because it worked for as long as my muscles could compensate for my deteriorating focus—that I still had the twenty-twenty eyesight of a decade ago. But the illusion was no longer working, my lenses were too far gone, and I had to get responsible. The nation's newspapers had not conspired against me to reduce the size of their print. . . .

What if all that energy I'd been pouring into that illusion of twenty-twenty eyesight had been free for other purposes? How much less tired would I have been? How many fewer mistakes would I have made over the years? How much money would I have saved on headache medication—how many headaches would I have avoided entirely? How many things would I have actually seen instead of having to guess?

When I got my glasses a week later, I was amazed to see how big Loki really is. Up until then, I'd seen him as a healthy-sized dog, but hardly as the imposing animal—"Da Moose" as my sister calls him—he actually is. At the other end of the spectrum, I suddenly could see the individual hairs of his coat and how subtly the different shades of his coloring blend together.

My alcoholic-addicted denial was much like my blurring eyesight. If you can't believe what you see, what can you believe? . . . especially if you've been told you've got twenty-twenty vision (albeit the last time a doctor told you that was ten years ago)? I believed my perception of me and my world when I was drinking and using because that's what the "lenses" of my perception and understanding made me see. What's more, the people around me, for the most part, perceived and understood as I did. (Maybe that's why they were *my* friends.) The cumulative, progressive effect of the deterioration was that my grasp of reality got more skewed, befuddled, and blurred as my denial became more habitual and deeply entrenched. And as is humanly normal, my emotional life danced the tune orchestrated by my perception and understanding and beliefs; I felt in accordance with what I saw.

If I saw something as funny, I laughed. If it was depressing, I shut down; if it was sad, I cried. The more I saw my world to be (pardon my French) fucked up, the more I responded emotionally to what I believed I saw—and by the time I hit bottom, I saw life to be nothing less than empty and hideously flat. Of course I was shut down and cynical! What the hell else could anyone be who saw and knew that truth?

It never occurred to me to have the "lenses" checked, to question the "eyesight" through which I was led to my understanding and interpretations. And since the people in my life (who mostly, just by the way, happened to be drinking buddies and/or codependents) confirmed my "vision," I rested secure. I believed I knew that I knew I was right.

The people of AA were the first to challenge that security and that vision of mine. At least they were the first ones I was able to hear; enough pain can make even the most bullheaded person willing to listen and reevaluate.

I don't romanticize my experience with AA or the other Twelve-Step programs with which I've been involved. All has not been sweetness and light. I've not taken easily or completely to the discipline. At various times, I've had my share of resentment and "philosophical" differences with Program people. In my cynical moments, I like to paraphrase Winston Churchill's remark about democracy: AA is really a wretched way to go about recovery; it just happens to be the best one we've got. For all of that, I've never lost that feeling of being "home" when I'm at a meeting.

One morning I heard a fascinating report on National Public Radio. Some sociologists on the East Coast were doing a study that evaluated the realism with which various groups of people saw world events. Intriguingly, the group that had, by far, the most realistic appreciation of our world's dynamics and antics was practicing alcoholics. They had no illusions left—"you can't bullshit the bullshitters."

I've no way to document that story or to check on the validity of the research that produced it. But even if the story isn't true, it should be. For, you see, a practicing drunk or junkie knows in his bones that life is, above all else, emptily absurd. What's more, if he's progressed to the latter stages of his chemical dependency, he not only knows it's absurd, he has no expectations that it should be otherwise. Given the follies of human history, that's pretty realistic.

I think our perception of the world's absurdity is one of the prime reasons we chemical dependents are so intractable. I'd thought of quitting my drinking and using several times before I actually hit bottom. Each time, the thought that gave me permission to use again was the question, "Why *should* I get sober? What difference would

The Heart of Surrender • 149

it make?" Nobody—no philosophy, no religion, no ethical system, no sense of social responsibility—could adequately answer those questions. There simply was *no good reason* to quit. My ideals had been scorched away.

So what was it that brought me to bottom, to the point that I'd even consider following the asinine instructions they shoved down my throat at my first meeting? Three things only: my emptiness, my exhaustion, and my pain. It didn't matter anymore that there was no good reason to get sober and straight. What did matter was that I simply hurt too much to continue going as I was going—I couldn't do it anymore. That's why I quit. That's the "reason" I stay quit.

Denial: A Way of Faith?

In the years since, I've reflected on my bottom experience again and again. Each time I ponder it (and reexperience it!), it gets richer. Much of that richness is personal and not for public consumption, but one of its elements I'm willing to share with you is what happened to my denial system during that time.

Belief systems—whether they be of the saint or the drunk—are powerful. They're wellsprings of action and the measures of our feelings of self-worth or guilt. They carry with them a sense of obligation. One of the more insane aspects of the latter stages of my drinking and using was the *sense of obligation* I felt to drink and use. Not only did I believe there was no reason to quit, I actually felt almost obliged to continue.

There is, I've found, a widespread presumption that chemical dependents are so clouded by their drugs that they don't know what they're doing or why. I believe the truth is almost exactly the opposite. We know precisely what we're doing, and are absolutely committed to doing it. We know how we're supposed to deal with any situation life tosses our way: We are *supposed* to drink and use. We're committed to doing what we're supposed to do with the kind of monomaniacal intensity that would shame a Jesuit questing for souls.

Not only could I not *not* use physiologically, I also felt a definite and distinct emotional obligation to continue. Others have told me that they, too, experienced the same internal demand. It may sound weird, but I almost felt guilty—as if I'd be living a lie—if I didn't drink and use.

In AA there's a saying that at one and the same time grated against my pride and hit home as only the truth can: "We drank because we were drunks." In the end, our drinking and using boiled down to a matter of being true to ourselves—a matter, if you wish, of ethics. That's what was so odd about those first AA meetings. They not only rebelled against my obligation, my ethic; they laughed at it. I actually think there was a part of me that suspected they were somehow dangerously *ir*responsible for going about their recoveries. I'd done a peace march or two in the 1960s and 1970s and always fancied myself a rebel, but this was too much. Who did they, society's obvious failures, think they were? They were the kind of people Momma had warned me about.

My reservations about their lack of ethics didn't disturb them very much, though. They just laughed again and told me to keep coming back. But my obligation to drink and use was overlaid with a second obligation: to deny that I was dependent.

Lord, how I fought in my denial—proving myself, proving my strength, proving my love, proving my competence, proving my goodness . . . proving my independence. But in the end, I always failed. Paradoxically, I failed precisely *because I proved* all those things I set out to prove: The more I proved, the more I could consider myself healthy, and the more (therefore) I deepened my denial. As a group, we addictive dependents are a bunch of tough, strong-willed, intelligent, overachieving, gifted people; we're survivors and we've *proved* it. Nonetheless, once the dust has settled and we've come full circle back to our pain, we all have to face the deadly and humiliating question, "So what?"

Pinning the Right Tail on the Right Donkey

When I first came into AA (and, if I'm honest, today, too), I had strong, "principled, intelligent" objections to the Program. Most of the time, other people at the meetings let me rant and didn't pay me much heed, other than an indulgent smile or two. Once, though, I got under an "old-timer" 's skin. He glared at me and snapped out this question: "Would you rather be right, or would you rather be happy?" I had to answer, "Happy." He responded, "Then shut up and follow directions. The only thing your intelligence and your 'right answers' got you was here. If you want a refund on your misery, go back out and do it your way." I shut up.

That was the key. I'd spent my life learning how to be right: think "right," do "right," and function "right." I'd had the best of good reasons for making all the choices I'd made. But I'd failed at the only thing life is truly about—living. The only thing being "right" had done was get me deeper into denial and pain. *Failure* is a devastating word, but I don't know of one that fits better.

I'm sure anyone working in recovery would agree that what's crucial to the healing process is that the chemically dependent person come to the point of saying and believing, "I just can't do it anymore, I'm finished." That recognition is the absolutely necessary linchpin of recovery. We cannot, we will not be able to, change until we face the truth: We've been beaten. We've failed.

I pound on this theme of failure for a reason. It's only when we've burned through all our resistance to the thought of being failures that, paradoxically, we can succeed in finding any peace. You see, denial and resistance (and failure) happen in the "head." More than any other part of us, our heads (and the committees convened inside of them) scream without letup that we're *not* beaten. They analyze, figure out, explain, and rail against the obvious. They do so at the chemical and physiological bidding of our dependency. As long as our dependency rests on its foundation of denial, we will be resistant to the truth of what our chemicals are doing to us; and so we can continue to partake of our drugs of choice. On the other hand, when that foundation cracks and collapses, we can finally face the agony of withdrawal and quit.

Our sense of failure has to be more than intellectual. Remember Alva's story about the two little boys and the test about the black rock: Understanding doesn't do it; we have to *know*. When we humans come to that kind of knowledge—whether it be "good" knowledge or "bad" knowledge—something inside of us (our soul, perhaps) finds quiet and peace.

An example: The rule of thumb when dealing with potential suicides is that you start to worry *not* when they're agitated but when they suddenly get calm and peaceful. All too often, that means they've finally made their decision to do "it." Likewise, research theorists and clients in therapy speak of the same sort of peaceful calm that hits them when an insight toward which they've been intensely striving finally falls into place. The last pieces of the puzzle come together and suddenly, overwhelmingly—in peace—we see. We finally *see*.

It's like my knowledge that I'm right-handed. I can give you all sorts of concrete evidence that that's true, but I "knew" it before I ever picked up a ball or a pen—it just was, and is, and will be, from the womb. And I know my right-handedness, not just in my head, but in every instinct and fiber of my being. That's the kind of knowledge I have today when I say I'm an alcoholic and addict, or when I acknowledge my failure.

Up to a millisecond before that intuition, before that knowledge snapped into place, to say and accept I was an addict and alcoholic—a failure—seemed *and felt* like the most stupidly suicidal thing I could do. A half-second afterward, it seemed *and felt* as though nothing else ever was or could have been true. That intuitive knowing made me different, and gave me peace.

Just Before Dawn

Sometimes the insight comes together in an instant. Sometimes it takes time. For me, it was a two-step process that went on for close to five months. I've already described how my head logically figured out (understood) that I was an alcoholic and got me into Guest House, and how rageful my alcoholic gut was when it found me stuck there in Michigan for the winter. (I've always been a person of delayed reactions; it takes my gut anywhere from five minutes to five months to catch up with my head.) For close to four months, I smoldered in that depressive rage, my head admitting I was alcoholic, my gut resisting it. All by myself, I was an emotional boxing match.

The bell rang about three-and-a-half months into treatment. It was the custom for Guest House priests to celebrate mass at neighboring treatment centers and to observe other addict/alcoholics during their early recovery process. It was while attending one of these group meetings as a nonparticipating guest that I suddenly understood. I can't recall that any of the discussion had any special impact, but at the end of the session I suddenly found myself saying—*with feeling,* "My God, I'm *sick!*"

Given the content of that realization, logic says I should have been devastated. Instead, I found myself finally, suddenly . . . relaxed, peaceful, almost floating. All the tension and resistance evaporated; I felt whole. I found myself smiling, and that night, for the first time since I came to Guest House, I slept like a baby. The war was over.

From today's vantage point, I have some clarity about what happened that weekend. There was an ironic, perhaps even hilarious, paradox about my realization and acceptance that I was a sick failure. For the first time, I'd successfully grasped my truth. I knew that I was knowing, with clarity and certainty, who and what I was; that was enough. I'd discovered my own secret; I'd taken possession of my truth; I'd finally owned myself. Previously, I'd only understood who I thought I was.

The psychiatrist at Guest House loved to boil things down to short, pithy sayings. One I'd been resisting and wrestling with now clicked home, "Everything that has happened should have happened." Before, I had seen the logic of what he said; now, it made sense *for me.* There were no accidents; *I was exactly who I was supposed to be, exactly in the place I should have been.* Instead of fighting with my truth and sinking in the quicksand of my denial, I relaxed and floated, and that's what I've done ever since.

What's different today is that *I know that I* don't *know.* With sobriety and recovery, the facts haven't changed. Man's inhumanity to man is no less real than before. My own brokenness and empty spots have not gone away. The idealistic romanticism my drugs and alcohol burned away has not returned. There is little in the way of human vagaries that could shock or surprise me.

Yet, today, I am different. All of those stark facts and squalid realities do not, today, lead me to join lockstep in the march to the sea of self-destruction as they once did. The world makes no more rational sense now than it did then, yet today I'm choosing—more or less bumblingly, with more clumsiness than grace—to live . . . and what's more, to enjoy my living.

When I was practicing my chemical addictions, my world made a kind of logical, if empty, sense, and my behavior fit within the scheme of that nonsensical world. I fit, and, in my depths, I knew it. There was a black harmony to it all. *"In vino veritas,"* the Romans used to say: "In wine, the truth."

Since I had no doubts, there was no reason to change. In fact, there was every good reason not to, for change would have been an act of stupidity.

With recovery's hindsight, I see that there was one small problem with that scenario: I was not God. For God to have such certainty, such sureness of self-possession, is only fitting; that's what it is to be divine. But for a human, for me or anyone else, it is just and only an act of arrogance.

The surrender to (and acceptance of) my chemical dependency upended my knowledge that I knew what "it" and I were all about.

Round and Round and Round

You see, I *was* right; I suspect every practicing addict and alcoholic is right about the world. But what recovery is teaching me is that "being right" is ultimately irrelevant.

"Would you rather be right, or would you rather be happy?" I was "right," true to my dependency, by continuing to drink and use. I was "right," true to my lifestyle, in being faithful to the behavior patterns of my alcoholism—isolating, lying, manipulating, cheating, etc., etc., etc. I was "right," true to my denial, in my despair and self-destruction. But being right damned near killed me: I was exactly who I was supposed to be; that was my problem.

The stick of verbal dynamite that exploded the certitude of my rightness was the statement by another recovering drunk, "You don't have to drink." Now, that was crazy! It was wrong: He was telling me I didn't have to do what I knew I *had* to do. It didn't make sense. It went against everything I understood and knew and believed. It contradicted my experience of myself. It was not right— *but it was true*.

All of my recovery has been like that. I was (and am) right in saying that chemical dependents like myself, whether practicing their dependency or recovering, are horribly self-absorbed, angry misfits. Therefore, it is right that I should isolate myself from them. Yet the truth is, I need them if I'm going to heal. Based on the evidence, it is right to conclude that life is an empty, meaningless, piteous endeavor; that good guys finish last; that might makes right; that Murphy's Law is the supreme truth; that the Constitution is what the Supreme Court says it is; and that war is the most efficient means of population control. Yet it is more deeply true that living is about compassion, and that the only fate worse than loving badly is not loving at all.

You see, in my denial, I lived with the presumption that being intelligent, being right, being rational, being "sensical," was what life was supposed to be about. I was sure that he who is right wins— even if it results in self-destruction—and that winning equals happiness.

Another way of looking at it would be to say that in my chemical dependency, I was well-adjusted, in sync. I was in harmony with the world's meaninglessness. I flowed along, unresistant to society's denial. Best of all, I could still look good doing it; the halo was tarnished, but I could (and did) pass off that dross as the patina of age, character, and the school of hard knocks.

Alva defines "adjustment" as "doing the breaststroke through a cesspool with a smile on your face because you haven't gotten any in your mouth—yet." I could still smile, and even crack a risqué joke with the boys once in a while. I fit. I knew my place . . . and I knew yours, too.

The cesspool was getting too wide, though, and, besides, I hurt. Being right and adjusted, even though it was right, was not working—and that was true.

Time and again, in treatment, therapy, and AA, I've seen other chemically dependent people push through the same process to own their truth. Sometimes quickly or sometimes slowly, sometimes in raging struggle or sometimes in quiet contemplation, the intuition, the realization, comes home to rest . . . and we change.

The peculiar thing about it is that everything changes, yet nothing changes. The physical circumstances of our lives remain the same; the wreckage from our drinking and using doesn't disappear; the physical distress of withdrawal continues; each of us, in his or her own way, is still tossed about in the craziness of the disease; yet somehow that's okay. It doesn't matter anymore. We're different.

There's a social dimension to the realization, too. Instead of seeing other chemically dependent people in a "me-them" light, I found myself talking in terms of "we." We only do to other people exactly what we're already doing to ourselves. When peace was declared in me, then and only then, at that moment of surrender and not a second before, I was at peace with others as well.

A Community of Faith

But surrender, like denial, has to become a way of life. Lest it seem that I suddenly found myself transplanted to some sort of emotional nirvana, I soon found out that acceptance and surrender are not once-and-for-all events; they're an evolving, growing process. My habit patterns and denial systems from twenty years' worth of chemically dependent drinking and using were not to be sloughed off quickly or easily. They'd embedded themselves much too deeply.

Too, I found in myself living proof of what they told me around the AA meetings, that I'd be chemically toxic for at least two years after I quit using. At regular intervals during those years, I went through what they called "chemical releases," which brought on periods of agitated depression and murky confusion. They'd last anywhere from a week to a month and shake me until my emotional eyeteeth rattled.

I discovered—much as the thought repulsed me—that I couldn't do recovery and sobriety all by myself, no matter how strong my initial, intuitive acceptance of my alcoholism. There are two fundamental ingredients to any belief system: One, they are habits; two, they are socially based. To change them, therefore, we have to introduce new counter-habits, and those new habits must find a social foundation of their own. Concretely, that meant I had to discover how to build a habit of sobriety, and I had to find a society that would give that new habit support, reinforcement, and validation. If I didn't, the new belief—for that's what this kind of total realization is—would be smothered and soon forgotten.

That's the reason I so emphasize the social dimension of denial. In the same way nobody can be an addict or alcoholic without social acceptance, enabling, and support, so nobody can long be in recovery from chemical dependency without a parallel kind of social acceptance, enabling, and support.

There's a last note about this idea of a community of support. At least ideally, I believe it needs to be composed of other people in recovery. I've found I just don't believe it when people who've not been there say things like, "I know how you feel," and "Trust me." I've been honored over the years to know some wonderfully warm and compassionate persons—Archbishop Hunthausen, for example. For all of their compassion, however, I've yet to meet one of them who knew—really knew—what chemically dependent people go through unless they'd personally been there. I'm not saying there could never be such a person, just that I've just not met one.

I was lucky. I was given the friends and community I needed in AA before I realized I needed them, people who accepted me precisely because of my unacceptability. With them in place, my own acceptance of my alcoholism—my surrender to failure—had the soil it needed to take root and grow. There were times I forgot the realization; they didn't. And because they remembered when I didn't, I got sober in spite of my confusion, pain, and recurring resistance. The foundation of peace, of knowing that I knew who and what I was—thanks to them—has never left.

Perspective

And finally there has been the laughter—not huge gales of it, more of a gentle undertone. There don't seem to be too many big deals anymore—at least when I'm living in my sobriety. That doesn't make much sense, since I'm as angry as I've ever been, and as scared and suspicious. For those things and people to which and with whom I've bonded, I'm as possessive and jealous as ever. I can still milk the last drop of bile out of a resentment, and bristle like a porcupine at criticism. And I can still do an emotional shutdown that'd put the Sphinx to shame.

But for all of that, something's different. All of those feelings and moods are simply part of the stuff of human life. If they happen, when they happen, they're not fun to undergo; they hurt. Yet, today, even their hurt can be welcome, not because I'm a masochist, but because they are an infallible sign to me that I'm alive. Before, I understood that but seldom felt it, and so I was hopeless.

So, today, my world's been stood on its head, and I find myself smiling at the most outrageous things, like near misses by speeding cars—not because they're near, but because they miss. Or my failures, because my pratfalls can be so slapstick. Or another drunk's horror stories, because we've both paid our dues and there's nothing left to prove.

The world's still absurd. The Holocaust happened, and it still has no meaning. Drunks and junkies heal, and that, too, makes no sense. Like Zorba the Greek, maybe we can come to know that life is about tears but that also it is about dancing—and that either reaffirms life, our longing and our hope.

Chapter 11

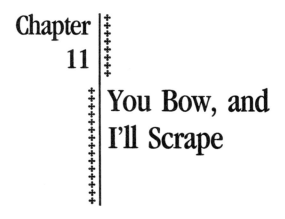

You Bow, and I'll Scrape

Re-Discovery of the Self
Hidden Behind Codependent Denial

Snapshots

Let me share three snapshots, as it were, that sum up the essence of codependent relationships.

My grandfather was an alcoholic; my grandmother belonged to the WCTU (Women's Christian Temperance Union).

Arnold, a client of mine, decided if he couldn't beat her, he'd join her, so he started drinking with his girlfriend. Eventually, he ended up in treatment—at which point she left him because she didn't want "to be involved with a drunk."

Loki, at times, with his muzzle stretched out on the floor, gazing up at me with what seem to be adoring eyes, appears to regard me as his "Higher Power."

———

My grandparents were at war. Arnold had no self-respect. Loki—translated into human terms—reminds me of the perfect "political wife," gazing on adoringly, mannequinlike, as her big, strong husband "speechifies" to the crowd.

How Do I Speak My Love?

Unfortunately, those three pictures remind me of myself. When I've been in love, the thought, the simple thought, that I might lose my beloved has made me feel as though I were going to die. And I'm reminded of the saying that Fred passed on to me and that I quoted in an earlier chapter: When we're in love ". . . it's like *we're* drowning and it's *their* lives that flash in front of our eyes."

The experience a codependent undergoes once Cupid's arrow strikes home is an unmatched example of the opposite of everything being true. Nothing gets more people into therapy; nothing triggers more confusion; nothing generates more tears—or rage; nothing causes more emotional devastation than codependent relationships. Equally, nothing's harder to get to, or more resistant to the healing process, than codependency. Today, I find it far easier to speak and write of my history as a drunk and prescription junkie than I do of my experiences at love and relationship.

Some of my reticence, I'm sure, flows from having been a priest and, therefore, committed not to get "involved" with anyone. Yet breaking those rules explains only a small percentage of my guilt and embarrassment: I've always had a quiet yet powerful streak of Puckish rebelliousness that delights in breaking rules. My reluctance to be open around this issue comes from something deeper and more potent than religious vows and ecclesiastical strictures.

Let me try to sketch the outline of my codependency in the following manner.

When I've found myself emotionally connected and bonded, a "tape" has automatically started to play. This tape has absolutely nothing to do with the people I've fallen for: who they are, what they've done or not done, how they've returned or rejected my love—that's all irrelevant. All the tape needs to get it going is my experience of bond*ing,* my *action* of clicking into "love mode." To state it another way, *whom* I love has next to nothing to do with *how* I love, *how* I relate.

Second, how I "do" my love is sick. It's sick because of my expectations; the most overwhelming assumption is that I must make my love my reason for living. It's sick because of the expectations I place on the loved ones, the most overwhelming of which is that I expect the ones I love must make me their reason for living, to love me as I love them.

It's sick because its deepest motivation is not freedom but fear. I would do anything, even enslave them, not to lose them. The last thing I'd dream of doing would be to offer them the nurturing acceptance and support that would enable them to live their own lives for their own sake, in freedom. My greatest concern is to get them to need me—whether or not they really want me.

It's sick because it's usually focused on a future "what could be" rather than a present "what is." If only they'd not drink so much, or be so absorbed in their work, or be more responsible, or love me the way I love them, etc.—our relationships would be perfect. If I could only please them more, or be more attractive and sexy, or earn more money, or relate to their interests more fully—things could be so good. In this kind of future-oriented equation, the only guarantee is that neither person in the relationship is ever "enough." My love always has more to do with potential than reality.

My love is sick because it propels me to get so enmeshed in my loves' lives (and demand that they get so enmeshed in mine) that we end up looking like emotional Siamese twins rather than partners bonded in and by respectful freedom.

My love is sick because it's so impersonal. This is how I love no matter who it is I love, when it is I love, or what the circumstances of our relationship may be—or how the loved one may feel about it.

My loving is sick, in short, because it intends to re-form my beloveds into my own image and likeness—or, at the very least, in the image and likeness of what I'm sure the loved ones should be.

They must love me as I love them, or else they really don't love me at all. I do relationships as power struggles; I always make my love conditional. I become so determined and so demanding of my partners that I have next to no chance to delight in and appreciate them for who they are. Loving and relating as I'm programmed to love and relate is a deadly serious business that leaves little time or room for spontaneity, fun, and play.

To sum it up, I do my loving—I'm programmed to do it—the way an alkie does his drinking or a junkie does his drugs. How do I love? Addictively . . . and therefore self-destructively, and therefore abusively.

In short, falling in love always got me angry—and I'm not talking irritated, I'm talking pissed.

But that was only the first half of the question. The second is when I'm in love, I'm bonded—in spite of myself. The interesting thing about bonding is that it happens with utter disregard for my intelligence or willpower or desire. Five minutes before I fall in love, I don't know it's going to happen. Five minutes after it's happened, I can't shut it off no matter how much I may decide I want to, or "understand" that I should. Bonding doesn't follow the rules of common sense or the canons of logic. It's like flypaper: The more I swat at it and fight it, the more I get stuck.

For those of us whose lives flow down the river course of denial, that double-pronged reality of our way of doing love (power struggles on the one hand, bonding on the other) makes for a most sorry state of affairs. Talk about "damned if you do and damned if you don't"! The more I see the negative and fight against it, the more my beloved fills my emotional horizon, and thus the more deeply bonded I become. But the more bonded I am, the more I become sensitive to and focused on the negative in the person of my beloved, and the more it rubs me raw.

I don't have too much experience with "healthy people" in relationship, but I suspect they are subject to the same potential for "push-pull" in their loves. But I also suspect they instinctively handle it first by surrendering to their bonding, then by focusing on the positive attributes of their loved ones and developing a more or less gentle sense of humor about the rest.

The operative word in that last sentence is *instinctively*. We codependent folk *instinctively* do the exact opposite; that's our problem. Because we live in denial, we first try to control the uncontrollable, namely our emotional bond, by denying its power. Then we focus on the negative and lose sight of the positive. It's a poor recipe for joy, companionship, play, contentment, and peace.

The last point, the keystone to codependency's subtle power, is one of the fundamental "givens" about being human: I, like every other man, woman, and child, am a social animal. I—even the chemically dependent part of me—can live without my drugs and alcohol. I can't live without you, though, nor you without me. Emotional bonding is not an accidental, incidental, secondary part of the human adventure. It comes with the territory; without it, we're either dead or psychotic; it's necessary.

Consequently, when I live in denial and fight against my bondedness, I've declared war on my own humanness, above and beyond whatever damage I may be wreaking on my beloved.

That's the scenario, the plotting of the drama. Its unfolding usually introduces one final ingredient to the emotional mess percolating to the surface—namely, guilt. When we battle against those we love, we hurt them—and for that we feel guilty. We may truly be unable to break off the battering and the attacks; we may be powerless over the tapes that force us to make nightmares of our relationships; but that inability, that powerlessness, is the last thing we're prepared to believe about ourselves. So we're convinced we could have done our loving differently, and we feel guilty.

In plain fact, we could not have done our loving differently. In plain fact, we loved in the only ways we knew how. And—like it or not, "admirable" or not—we have functioned to the best of our abilities in this terrifying game and have done nothing we ought to feel guilty about—horrified, yes, but not guilty. Of course, we feel guilty nonetheless.

Such is the pickle of codependent relationships. They hurt like hell because they bring us face-to-face with the dimensions of ourselves we least want to confront. They render us desperate, confused, consumed with angry resentment, feeling empty and, worst of all, feeling needy. They devour our emotional resources; they leech from our souls any sense of self-possession and centeredness.

It would seem logical, given all that painful craziness, to swear off relationships altogether. Some of us try that, but it seldom works. The sad fact is that we're drawn to relationships like moths to flame; we are human. . . . All too often our lives seem too empty to be borne in solitude. We don't feel alive unless we're "connected." The pain of our way of loving is still preferable to the emptiness of going it alone.

Once Again, Surrender

As with recovery from chemical addiction, so for recovery from emotional dependency. The first step is facing the truth and speaking it—surrender. And that feels no less stupid and suicidal for co-dependents than it does for addicts and alcoholics.

I can remember driving home one Christmas Day several years ago so absorbed in my speeding mind and churning gut, so caught up in the pain of my relationship, that I'd blacked out on the distance and time I'd been traveling. Every voice in my head's "committee of denial" screamed I really wasn't dependent, that I didn't really need my beloved, that I'd die if I gave in to my neediness. Then, out of the blue, much like the intuition that came about my chemical dependency, I found myself saying out loud, "But I *am* dependent."

My gut unwound, my head shut up, I was suddenly able to see the road before me, and I began to smile. The paradox of my surrender to chemical dependency was that once I owned I was an addict-alcoholic, I no longer had to be victimized by it. So, too, for my emotional dependency. In the same way that it was my denial about being chemically dependent that was killing me, it was my denial about my emotional dependency that was ripping me to shreds. I found that when I accepted my bondedness, then, for the first time, I felt free to make some choices about it—like was this relationship good for me, did I really want to invest my time and energy in this person? For the first time, I was able to face the price I'd have to pay for staying in this relationship, and the price, too, of breaking it off—the loss of personal independence in the former case, grief and loneliness in the latter.

It seems my codependent denial, like the denial of my other dependencies, had me doing my life "bass-ackward." The one thing that was most true and most obvious, my emotional bonding, was the one thing I denied and resisted most fiercely. I fought to insulate myself from the intensity of the feelings that flowed from that bonding, be they positive or negative. For if I could numb those feelings and thus escape their jerking me around, I could then run my emotional life from my head and be in control. Finally, then, I believed that if I was in control, I was powerful.

I'd never learned that control is the exact opposite of power; for, if power is the acquisition and ownership of options, control is their expenditure. Every time I exert control over my feelings and over the ones I love, I expend more of my options and get that much closer to emotional bankruptcy. Conversely, every time I relax into acceptance and let go, I preserve my options and deepen my power, my ownership of my own life.

And I choose to live in acceptance if and when I choose to live in trust. That's the rub—for how can I trust when I'm so vulnerable to my beloved? She or he can hurt me like nobody else. The only logical, rational thing, then, is to get more guarded and mistrusting as I get closer and more bonded.

Fortunately or unfortunately, trust is not a rational virtue like justice. Justice is giving to people what they deserve, whereas trust and hope mean nothing unless they mean "hoping when everything is hopeless," as Chesterton said.

From that, I take it that trust is a choice before it's a feeling; and that its rewards come not so much from the response of the one trusted as from the giving of the trust itself. Such an attitude is not logical, and it is the furthest thing from a codependent's manipulative and controlling mind; yet it is the only thing, paradoxically, that works.

My friend Andy told me a story about his bottom that illustrates the point. For years, his mother had cajoled and shamed him about his drinking and using, to no avail. One night, though, when he'd passed out drunk on the living-room floor, she just spread a blanket over him and put a pillow under his head. When he woke up and saw what she had done, it was as if all the pressure came off. He felt as though he was accepted, that, as he said, "It was okay." Soon after he got sober.

Perspective

Let's go back to the snapshots that began this chapter.

War between couples, enmeshment to the point of self-dissolution, and partners placed on divinizing pedestals are examples of codependent extremes. They're the stuff of soap-opera melodrama; yet, too, they're the ordinary, daily script of addictive dependent love affairs. In the long run, they can only be suicidal, screened as they are by denial and fantasy.

Maybe if we look at Loki as he is—that is, as a dog and not as a human being driven by human motivations and rationalizations—we can come up with a metaphor about healthy relationships.

He can wheedle and manipulate and control, but the one thing he can't do is denial. He's very relaxed about his emotional dependency; I get the distinct impression he believes it is what should be. To tell the truth, he probably could get along without me; he is beautiful enough and engaging enough to entice somebody else to be his human if the need should arise. As well, tame animals can go feral if they must to survive. But it's pretty obvious he's satisfied with things as they are. Even when I'm grumpy or distracted, he stays close and behaves as if the glass is always at least half full.

Strangely enough, his dependency seems to give him independence in the rest of his life. He seems very free to choose for himself how he will relate to other humans. He picks and chooses with whom he's going to be affectionate or with whom he will be standoffish; and he doesn't seem to feel obligated by the wishes of those other humans. Just because *they* want to be his friends isn't reason enough in itself for *him* to accept their overtures. He always seems to have the independence to honor his own feelings in the matter. What his criteria for human associations are, I'm not quite sure—but they're definitely there, and definitely his own. The dysfunction is not in the dependency but in the denial.

For us codependents, love relationships and the dependencies that inevitably accompany them are scary and threatening. So, much as we want them, we fight against them, and thus become victims of our loves.

If there is a solution to that dilemma, it is to be found in the same paradox chemical dependents must pass through if they are to heal. We codependents, too, must learn to surrender to our dependency. In that surrender—and only there—our paranoia can dissolve, our tension can relax, and our human truth can find the courage to share itself in love.

Chapter 12

Sticks and Stones Will Break My Bones, but the Truth Will Never Touch Me

Breaking Through ACOA Denial

All of my recovery has been a series of comeuppances. Again and again, my powerful and sophisticated brain has found itself confounded by the simple and the obvious. Despite my finely tuned education, I seem to have made it my life's pattern to be blind to those things in myself a child could not help but see. Like: If you drink the way I did, you're a drunk; and if you love the way I do, you're sick.

But nowhere have I viewed my life more through the wrong end of the telescope than in my understanding of how my childhood formed and programmed me. Since I presume you may have had the same difficulty, let me forewarn you that this chapter on the ACOA healing process will challenge you to lay aside your "adult" beliefs and prejudices so that you might once again see with the eyes of a child.

I guarantee that the mature and grown-up part of you will not enjoy the exercise. If you identify with what I have to say, you will probably feel foolish, embarrassed, and ashamed. If that happens, good; for you'll be on the only sane path to your truth.

Twice while teaching my Adult Children of Alcoholics course, I've been embarrassed because I unexpectedly choked up and started to cry. Both times I was speaking of my own childhood.

It first occurred as I speculated about the emotional trauma I believe I went through as a child to survive the impact of my father's death and my mother's consequent shock at his passing. He was an engineer in Platinum, a mining camp on the western edge of the Kodiak Peninsula. With no warning, at age forty, his heart stopped one day as he drove his truck to work. The picture I've been given is of the three of us flying out to Anchorage in a bush plane, my father lying in his coffin down the center aisle; and my mother holding me, her four-month-old baby, seated beside her husband's body.

I can't imagine how stunned my mother must have been, how numbed with shock she must have become just to survive, function, and take care of both of us through all of that. And until that day in class, I had no memory or any idea other than hypothetical of how I'd coped. I was illustrating to my students that in trauma such as I'd experienced infants have only three options. Because their emotional systems are so undeveloped, they die, go insane, or withdraw almost totally into themselves in the face of emotional catastrophe. I compared those of us who withdrew to autistic children, kids who have next to no sense of the reality of the world about them. (I saw one wander into the middle of a busy arterial once; he had no fear, no sense of danger as the cars whizzed and swerved by.) As I talked about that withdrawal, about how close to a kind of autism some of us had to skirt just to survive, I choked up and started to cry.

The second time for tears came as I talked about the lasting nature of childhood hopes and dreams. Two or three months prior to that class, I'd been intensely, forcibly reminded of one of mine: As a kid, one of my great hopes was to have a puppy of my own. How deep that desire had been hit home over the course of a coincidence-packed day. I'd arrived at the college ten minutes or so before my class in order to stop by the office to get my mail. Two of the department secretaries were on the floor playing with a white and fawn Great Dane puppy; he couldn't have been more than a couple of months old. They'd found him that morning, sniffing around the garbage can by the rear door of their office. He was skinny, collarless, and wonderfully winsome, so they brought him inside, sent somebody to get him food, and were discussing what to do with him as I entered. Neither of them could possibly take care of him, either as a puppy or especially as the giant-sized pooch he'd soon become. Naturally, the idea of calling the Humane Society surfaced. Something inside of me balked at that, so I suggested they feed him and then bring him to my classroom. I'd see if any of my students would take him.

Ten or fifteen minutes after class began, there was a knock on the door, and in came the head secretary, puppy in tow. The students immediately took to him, and vice versa. He scampered up to every person in the room, sniffing, licking, wiggling, and wagging. But he kept coming back to me. By the time the period ended, he was snuggled asleep in the crook of my left arm. I wanted him—but: I was settling into my new home; he'd get too big; he'd eat too much, etc. . . . All the grown-up, rational, adult reasons you can think of sizzled through my brain to get me to say no. Besides, there was a woman in the class who wanted him for her two little children. I gave her the puppy.

Later that afternoon, I went to visit a friend of mine who raises exotic goldfish. One of them, a koi, had died. For some reason, I decided to stop at the local pet store to get her another, which I duly delivered.

Finally, that evening I went to my regular Al-Anon meeting. I was the first invited to speak, and I gave an innocuous little report on my week that said in sum that everything was "fine." (In my part of the country, we've a saying that the word *fine* is actually an acronym for "Fucked up—Insecure—Neurotic—Evasive.") But after I spoke, I felt myself suddenly dropping into depression. I didn't know why; I couldn't think of any reason for feeling like that. I got up, ostensibly to get some coffee, but really in order to catch my breath and figure out what was going on. As I stood at the stove, filling my cup, the meaning behind my emotions came clear. As a little boy, more than anything I'd wanted my own puppy, but for good, sound, "sensical" reasons such as the smallness of the homes we lived in and the expense involved, I never got one.

That day, for exactly the same sort of "good reasons," I'd given away a puppy I wanted and who wanted me. What's more, I'd found a pet for someone else and had given it to her. I'd taken care of everyone else (the puppy, the secretaries, my student and her two kids, my friend), and ignored the hopes of the person closest to me (my own child).

That insight literally staggered me, and I rushed back to the meeting to share it. As I spoke the second time, and told my story, I choked up. And as I repeated the story of that day to my class, I started crying again.

Until those experiences, even though I intellectually grasped the idea of "the child within" that so many people in ACOA speak of, I don't think I really, gut-level believed in it. After all, it does sound a bit sappy and sentimental—especially for a grown-up man in a grown-up world. Besides, I'm a therapist, and isn't the goal of recovery and therapy to finally get mature and responsible, rather than stay regressed in infantile fantasies and childish dreams?

The opposite of everything is true. Once again, the workings of my own journey turned my world upside down and sent me back to the drawing board.

Let me backtrack a little. When I got about three years clean and sober, I found myself in a disconcerting emotional state. I'd detoxified, I'd built a strong recovery program, I had an excellent sponsor and a wonderful support group of friends; yet my life still didn't feel as though it was working. I had no zest; everything felt flat and empty. It wasn't that I *hurt;* I just felt empty. I was depressed.

Awareness of that depression took a while to sink in, but eventually my listlessness and flattened mood became undeniable. Today, I've come to understand that my depression had probably been going on for years, but that it had been masked and anesthetized by my chemical abuse. (Paradoxically, I used chemical depressants to numb out the emptiness of my depression. That may not sound rational to normal folk, but I'll bet there are a lot of addicts and alcoholics—as well as workaholics, overeaters, etc.—who identify.)

But by that time, I knew that I hadn't got sober to be miserable, so I decided to start therapy once again. For over two-and-a-half years, at first once a week, later twice a week, in individual sessions and in group, I talked and talked, and processed and processed, and felt and felt. It paid off, but it wasn't fun.

I read books like Alice Miller's *Drama of the Gifted Child*,[1] Claudia Black's *It Will Never Happen to Me*,[2] and Sheldon Kopp's *If You Meet Buddha on the Road, Kill Him!*[3] I went to ACOA meetings and listened to tapes by speakers like Bob Earll and attended workshops on dysfunctional and chemically dependent families. Most of all, through it all, when I realized what I was doing and also when I didn't, I grieved.

I'm willing to go only so far in this exercise of "show-and-tell." In spite the anecdotes I've shared in this book, I'm not an emotional exhibitionist, so the specifics and details of my therapy will remain private. Besides, I couldn't tell them if I wanted to. I've experienced one of the phenomena Freud said was indicative of a good therapy process: I've already forgotten most of it. Suffice it to say that I came away from it convinced of the observation made by a therapist friend of mine: Therapy is nothing short of a guided, slow-motion breakdown.

If I were to distill out the essence of that time and give a bottom-line summation of what it was all about, though, I think I'd have to say it was about three things: letting go, letting go, and letting go.

Here again, the fundamental dynamic was exactly the same one I'd faced in my recovery from chemical dependency and codependency. Once more I had to surrender; once more I had to face a bedrock-solid belief system of denial; and once more I had to come to know—not understand, but *know*—that I'd failed.

---

[1] Alice Miller, *The Drama of the Gifted Child* (New York: Basic Books, 1981).
[2] Black, op. cit.
[3] Sheldon B. Kopp, *If You Meet the Buddha on the Road, Kill Him!* (New York: Bantam Books, 1981).

Survival Gear

So, to heal, we must find a way to get "little" once again. We must touch into the pain of our childhoods and rediscover once more in our hearts just how bad it really was.

That goes against our deepest grain, for in the midst of our confusion and denial we ACOAs still know one thing about ourselves: We're survivors. Of that we've no doubt. It's our boast and, for many of us, our single pride. Damnably, though, it's also the cornerstone of our dysfunction.

One of the women in my ACOA class, a little spitfire, scarcely five feet tall, went into a rage as I described the abuse children of alcoholic families must endure. My point was that those of us raised in such homes were truly victimized (children *are* the only real victims). Her face got chalky white, and she began to tremble. I asked her what was wrong, and she fairly spat back the reply, "I don't, I *won't,* see myself as a victim!" All I could respond was, "But you are . . . but you *are!*" She started to sob.

Later on, I got to know her not only as a student, but also as a client. The story of her childhood and teenage years was horrifying, the struggle of her recovery amazing—a powerful testimony to the angry strength of her spirit. But precisely because of her determination in recovery and her stubborn reconstruction of her life, she'd been able to stay in denial about the lasting effects of her family's abusiveness: "It really hadn't been that bad." She'd survived, and so, today, with enough comprehension, work, and courage, she could have control (she implicitly believed).

Yet her life wasn't working. Her track record in personal relationships was horrendous, despite her innate attractiveness, and she had a brittle edge that kept the people around her on guard. She was always wound too tight.

She's not alone, either, in her ongoing dysfunction, or in her fierce resistance to her powerlessness in the face of childhood's lasting imprints. We *did* survive, says our logic, so it could *not* have been that bad.

What's more, even if we become inclined to see our childhoods for the hells they were, all too many of us look around and see others who had it "so much worse than we." So again we can (and do) conclude that what we went through couldn't have been *that* bad. And, of course, we wouldn't want to be self-pitying, would we?

Jewish people have a tradition of praying the Kaddish for the dead. In Jerusalem, they do it before the Wailing Wall. The great fear is that one will die so alone and unremembered that there'll be no one to sing the prayer. They know that the greatest sin is to forget.

But forgetting is what ACOA denial is all about. Santayana is supposed to have said, "Those who forget the lessons of history are doomed to repeat it." As for national histories, so for individual histories. If we forget our abusive childhoods, we're doomed to repeat them—in our own lives and the lives of our children. The simple fact is that we regard and treat ourselves as we have been taught, as we believe we should be regarded and treated—and we believe that we should be abused as our "gods" (Mommy and Daddy) have abused us.

Nor does it matter if we hate our parents and what they did to us. It does not matter if we have deliberately chosen not to be like them because—almost inevitably with that kind of choice—we will go to the opposite extreme in our determination to avoid resembling them. You might compare it to the two constituents of a photograph: If our parents are the "negative," we become the "positive." They may be "black" where we are "white," and vice versa; nonetheless, it's the same picture, the exact same picture.

For example: My compulsive-gambler stepfather, the Scapegoat son in his own dysfunctional family, was a Chicago Irishman with two moods, black rage and black depression. I clearly remember promising myself one day when I was about ten, after one of his blowups, that I'd never—*never*—get angry like him. And I didn't. In situations where he would have got angry, I got "nice." I got so nice that I didn't lose my temper more than three or four times between then and my forty-second birthday. But "depression," as the saying goes, "is anger turned inward," and did I ever get depressed! Later, in group therapy, my counselors and fellow clients kept chipping away at me, trying to trigger my anger. At last they succeeded, and I blew—like Vesuvius. I didn't get physically abusive, but, like my stepfather, I got roaringly loud and verbally cutting. It was so intense that three of the group had to leave the room, even though my rage wasn't aimed at them.

Once I calmed down, the thing that I found most terrifying, most shaming, was how much I looked and sounded like him—the only man I've ever hated. The one man from whom I wanted to be most different—at the one point when it was most important—was the one man I was most like. It took three months to work through my guilt about that one! (It does make a kind of sense after all: He *was* my role model for male anger.)

I'm a survivor and a victim, too. I, too, was not going to be held captive by my past. I could make myself into whom I wanted to be. But in that, too, I had failed.

Getting Plucked

It fits here to refer back to the story in Chapter 5 of Stalin and his plucked chicken. The horror of that episode lies not so much in the physical brutalizing the bird received as in the overwhelming rape suffered by its spirit. Its sense of itself was so flooded and submerged under the presence of its tormentor that it ended up emotionally possessed by the very person who'd tortured it. Stalin, in his ruthlessness, made himself the chicken's "Higher Power," its god. That fate is the lot of children in chemically dependent and dysfunctional families. Sometimes it happens in the brutality of chemically induced batterings; sometimes it happens in the smothering "love" of parents who force the child to make them its very reason for living; and sometimes it happens when parents so withdraw that children constantly dwell in a life-threatening terror of abandonment. In each case, children learn—intuitively, irrevocably, with utter certitude—their total dependence on Mommy and Daddy. Mommy and Daddy are their "Higher Power"; they bounce at the end of Mommy and Daddy's emotional yo-yos. From that moment on—either in conformity or reaction—they are *possessed* by their parents. As Stalin overwhelmed the emotional horizon of his chicken, these parents flood over the psyches of their kids, and thus come to own them.

So we were and we remain victims; the theme of our lives is survival. We become paranoid, ever on guard, never ceasing to hunt for some way, some foolproof formula by which we can control the circumstances of our lives, and we search, too, for some absolute security that might keep us from ever being enslaved like that again. But in that very quest for absolute security, we doom ourselves to spend our lives going from carbon copy to carbon copy of Mommy and Daddy . . . for, paradoxically, it is only one like those who so filled our spirits in the first place who can give us once again a sense of rock-solid security.

That's the flip side of emotional slavery and victimhood: In being the victim there's complete safety, because there's no risk or responsibility. All we have to do is *play by the rules* (namely, be the victims we're supposed to be, *as* we're supposed to be, *when* we're supposed to be) and we shall be secure. And that security is very real: Hegel and Marx saw clearly that masters need their slaves more than slaves need their masters. Indeed, they need our survival more than we do; for, without us, over whom would they be "divine"? Our gods, in their need (to maintain their "divinity") will keep us secure—and we know it. That's the final reversal of the plot: Our "gods" need us more than we need them. In the last analysis, we see ourselves in our heart of hearts as "more divine" than they: the greater the victimhood, the greater the "ego."

That's our dilemma. Much as we may hate and fear our victimhood, freedom and its risks seem even more frightening . . . not to mention "de-divinizing." It's the politics of fascist dictatorships sketched small, but no less real. Alice Miller[4] writes that if Hitler had been married with children, there would have been no World War II and no Buchenwalds. She doesn't exaggerate. Likewise, it's the politics of "trickle-down economics," patriarchies (and matriarchies), the Gulag, and fanatical fundamentalisms—secular or religious. The trade-off of responsible freedom for security and the illusion of divinity is pervasive; and its roots are to be inevitably found in the original, the smallest society, the family.

Weekly, I speak with client after client who says, "I want to get rid of my depression," or, "I don't want to be so sickly dependent

---

[4]Miller, op. cit.

in my relationship," or, "I want to be free." And weekly, as I hear them speak, a small (possibly cynical?) little voice inside me silently replies, "Wanta bet?" Despite my cynicism, though, they begin the journey, and a surprising number of them persevere.

As they begin, they start their first lesson in the opposite of everything being true. What usually brings them to offices like mine is pain; they're "sick and tired of being sick and tired." So they believe they need to find some way to stop the pain. They believe they shouldn't hurt. Strangely enough, though, the belief that they shouldn't hurt is the heart of their denial, and the source of nine tenths of their pain.

In fact, we are exactly who we are supposed to be. Given who we are, where we have come from, and how we've got where we are, we should not do anything else but hurt. Sometimes immediately, more often gradually, that paradox sinks in, and we learn the first and greatest bit of denial that has been the foundation for the rest of our addictive lives. You see, battering hurts, terror of abandonment hurts, being emotionally raped and possessed hurts; therefore, we struggle to discover the rules of the game precisely to control and anesthetize the pain of those hurts. Security for us, we believe, is the lack of pain.

What nobody taught us was that, safe as it seems, the security of emotional dependency is like the Chinese water torture. In the beginning, it doesn't hurt, and it can even seem pleasant; but in the end, its cumulative effect is to generate a pain that floods over all other sensations.

But we were children when we began our courses in survival, and children tend to generalize. We devised an all-inclusive rule, a belief, based upon what seemed to work for us in very specific circumstances. Because it seemed to work for us then, because it seemed to stop or control the pain of our childhoods, we came to believe that if we always "play by the rules," we should never hurt— at least not as much.

What works with one pain should work with another (a child believes); in for a penny, in for a pound. So, down the line, when as an adult my world collapses and I hurt like never before, I finally swallow my pride (because there's no alternative) and *do what I'm supposed to do,* ask for help. Once more, I play by the rules and I believe that, because I do, I should stop hurting. But, in fact, the denial is still running my life: With the best of intentions, I do the right thing for the wrong reasons—and the battle is joined. I seek help because I believe I should not hurt; but the first truth I must face is that I *should* hurt exactly and precisely with the pain I feel— for my pain is my only real assurance that I'm alive. The opposite of everything *is* true.

Another way of describing it is to compare ourselves to satellites launched from earth. We've used the energy of our fear or hate or anger to push ourselves away from Mother/Father Earth. Some of us orbit high, some low; we think ourselves free because we made it into space. But our orbits inevitably decay, slowly or quickly. We make corrections; we fire retrorockets; we claw to stay up; but eventually we fail and fall. The power of their "gravity" is greater than the energy of our determination to break free. All they have to do is stay put and let us waste all our energy trying to fight them.

However we characterize or exemplify the ACOA state of affairs, however unique our individual stories, the basic plot of our lives is the same. In the total dependency of our infancies and childhoods, we were brutalized. So, universally, we reached the only conclusion that, as children, we could reach. Since Mommy and Daddy are our gods, and since gods can't be or do "wrong," that brutalizing victimhood we experienced must be *our* fault, the result of something *we've* done; it must be what we *deserve*. Since the only thing we really did to get abused was to be dependent (as if we had a choice), what was and is "wrong," "bad," and "shameful" is just that—our dependency. So we hone our skills at control and we play by the rules in order to feel and believe one thing, and one thing only: We are no longer dependent. Dependency is bad; dependency is the enemy. That's our intuition, our logic, our strategy—our denial, and our pain.

But I Don't Want to Hurt

Pain's what all those roles ACOAs played (which we discussed in Part 1) are about. They're developing, ongoing scenarios by which we try to manipulate and establish some illusion of control over those who hold us in their power and inflict pain. *They are ever-continuing efforts by which we deny our dependency.*

Maybe the point will become clear if we contrast the roles children of alcoholic families play against those acted out by children of healthy families. In relatively healthy homes, children play exactly the same roles as the kids in alcoholic/dysfunctional families play. The differences, however, are that healthy kids play those roles for different reasons and with nowhere near the single-minded intensity we do. Healthy kids develop them as tools to help them establish their public identities, identities that are nurtured and supported by their parents and siblings but that are not seen to be the total expression of those kids' personalities.

Healthy, secure parents, in fact, rejoice as their children grow and find their independent selves. After all, that's what parenting's all about. Good parenting, like good teaching, is about getting out of children's lives as soon as possible so that they may assume responsibility and freedom for themselves. The point is to get the kids ready to fly from the nest.

At the same time, though, healthy families are also about each of the family members—parent or child—being able to relax and be vulnerable with one another. Instead of being on guard, they can be themselves whether or not they happen to be living up to their roles at any given minute. The Hero can come home and get little; the Lost Child can become outgoing; the little one can assume the lead; and the black sheep can even be loving and loved.

In alcoholic families, children play their roles to establish their identities, too.[5] But, in stark contrast to what happens in healthy homes, those identities are always assumed and acted out, not as expressions of a growing self-possession, but as ongoing manipulations of Mommy and Daddy. They are not about developing and

---

[5]To be more precise, the primary ACOA role is "Survivor." The various expressions of that primary role are the various images of "Hero," "Mascot," etc. These secondary roles can be rotated if the need arises. For example, an eldest child may die; often enough number two-child, to this point a Scapegoat, will suddenly take over the Hero job, and in the same manner the other siblings "move up." As well, although most of us "major" in one role, we can "minor" in any or all of the other roles if survival so demands.

growing up into one's own public person; they are about controlling and defusing parents. They're about emotional slavery rather than the establishment of emotional independence.

The kids in alcoholic dysfunctional families have to play their roles twenty-five hours a day. Heroes *always* have to be big; Mascots *always* have to be little; Lost Children *always* have to disappear; and Scapegoats *always* have to be angry. That word *always* is the key to the matter. When you're playing a role *all* the time, when you *never* dare let down your guard, you have no chance and no experience of being open and vulnerable. Instead of being a tool for getting along in the world, a tool that can be set aside when we're at home, the ACOA role becomes a snare in which one is inescapably trapped.

When we dig behind the act of those ACOA roles, then, and see them as expressions of denial, it's clear that what they deny is our dependency, our powerlessness in the face of our parents' domination.

But since dependency is one of the core constituents of intimate relationships, the very fact that we ACOAs play our "antidependency" roles so constantly—that we're so totally addicted to them—blocks us from truly achieving what our humanity most desires. Damned if we do and damned if we don't!

Push it further yet. To be human is to be dependent, is to be needy. For example, I need you for the language I speak; this world for the air I breathe and water I drink; and everybody and everything I ever meet to have a developing sense of my own self. To be truly independent would be to be self-sufficiently divine—and I ain't made it . . . yet.

So to deny my dependency is to deny my humanity; or viewing things through the other end of the telescope, to live in the belief that I am always able to be in control is to implicitly claim "I'm God." That may seem like an obtusely theological point to push—until you see its implications. Gods may love human beings, but they don't fall *in* love with us. The intensity of their flame would so engulf us that we'd burn to a crisp.

Or, as the Bible says, gods are jealous; they do not brook rivals. So if one "ACOA god" were to fall in love with another "ACOA god," could the result be anything else than a titanic power struggle and war between "divinities?"

Gods are splendid and omnipotent, but they are also isolated and alone. Whether they are gentle and humble in their ways or arrogant and demanding, they have to stand above and apart. Others may belong to them, but never they to others.

Thus, to survive we had to deny our dependency; but in denying it, we had to lose faith in the one thing that could give us life . . . our humanity, our child.

People from more or less healthy families look forward, I observe, to the dependency of love. Their experience of it in childhood was nurturing, warm, playful, freeing. They accept and enjoy their dependency and humanity as the creative source of their lives and happiness. I've yet to meet an ACOA who felt that way.

As with chemical dependency and codependency, *the* recovery issue is breaking through the denial by surrendering. If the truth be told, our dependency won't kill us, but our denial will—yet that's the exact opposite of what we believe.

I've Not Yet Begun to Fight.

So what does surrender look and feel like for the ACOA? After more clients than I wish to count and a longer personal journey than I ever dreamed of undertaking, I'm convinced the heart of ACOA surrender is the rediscovery of the child. Back there, in the mists of your and my beginnings, our children had to go into hiding to survive. They hid themselves so well that they hid themselves even from themselves, from us. For some of us it began when we were four months old; for others it happened at two or three or four years of age; but whenever it was, our kids went underground, deep—and they zipped the foxholes shut behind them.

If you want a demonstration that I'm not speaking in syrupy platitudes, get two pictures of yourself—one of when you were about two or three, and another of when you were anywhere from ten to twelve. Cover the photos except for the eyes and compare them. If you're like most ACOAs I know, the ten-year-old's eyes will stand out because of what's missing, namely sparkle and spontaneity. When we were still very young, our eyes danced like other kids' eyes. But once we'd got to ten or twelve (for most of us), our guards were up and our roles were locked in place. It shows.

Another way of finding out how deeply we've buried our children is to recall the times we've got most embarrassed, or felt most ashamed, or judged ourselves most guilty. In healthy people, those emotions are usually appropriate interior warnings that they're trespassing on propriety or morality. For us, though, they have much more to do with survival than morality. Again and again in therapy—my own and my clients'—I've observed that we get embarrassed, ashamed, or guilty when we find ourselves doing things which make us look foolish and vulnerable—childlike. That's what's most "wrong" and "immoral" for us—to be foolish, to get caught with our pants down, to give somebody else an opening they could use to criticize or judge us. In short, we get guilty, embarrassed, and ashamed when we set ourselves up to get caught. If and when "they" see us for who we really are (childish and needy), they'll mock us, and look down on us, and laugh at us, and not take us seriously, and judge us to be "not enough." And then—when they see us for who we really are—they'll punish us and abandon us. That's what our kids experienced and what they believe, so what else should they do but get hidden and stay hidden? What else is there to do but spend our days and our years playing "Let's Pretend" (as Bob Earll called it) to survive?

Adults, it seems, have to choose to play; they have to think about it. Kids just do it. They imagine and wonder and squeal and delight spontaneously. Given a modicum of security and a context of acceptance, they flow; they don't short-circuit their feelings through their brains. If they know they're loved without condition, they don't embarrass or worry about being appropriate. If they don't have to live constantly *en garde,* they question and explore, they lust for the new and wonderful.

If you're from an alcoholic or otherwise dysfunctional family, you may think such a rosy picture of childhood only exists in some romantic fantasy . . . that I've lost touch with reality. To be honest, I almost wish you were right. Indeed, if those few sentences about unobstructed childhood were nothing more than a fantasy, it would make the brutality of the world easier to deal with: Those who died with the most toys *would* win; success would be measured by our skill at manipulation; and our emotional health could be determined by our ability to adjust. All things we ACOAs rail against would instead be normal, and the name of the game *would be* "Survival."

Based on results, however, our version of maturity and adulthood and the meaning of life doesn't work—else I wouldn't be writing and you wouldn't be reading this book. By process of elimination, the only "place" we can turn for recovery, then, is back to the beginning, back to the child.

But that's a challenge and hard work: There's nothing more patronizing, nothing phonier, than an adult acting at being a child. We don't "get to" our children by reasoning and by choosing in an adult fashion to act like a child. In fact, the key to getting in touch with our children is becoming willing to be *really* irrational and *really* foolish . . . like a kid. Anyone who playacts at being a child does not take children seriously and respectfully.

Piaget and others have shown that rationality and the ability to conceptualize do not occur in children's lives until they are about seven or eight. Before that, kids live and know on an emotional-intuitive level. Consequently, if we are going to take our interior children seriously, we must, above all else, be willing to accept them for who they are and expect them to be nothing more—kids; emotional, intuitive, prerational kids.

In short, getting in touch with our children and taking them seriously means becoming willing to live in our feelings, unfiltered and uncensored by our adult intellects. For the children are the seat and the source of emotional life.

We have to reexperience the feelings of the child, the feelings that we stuffed "way back then" and against which we instituted our whole system of denial in the first place. When we actually were children, to live unguardedly in our childishness was life-threatening. Since kids have very little idea of time (it's an adult concept, after all), they don't know that today isn't yesterday. They just know that to let their guard down (to let go of their survival role) is dangerous. It was dangerous yesterday, so it's dangerous today, and will be dangerous tomorrow. No way are they going to relax and let down their defenses—and trust us—just because we say we want them to, or bribe them with a teddy bear or two. These kids aren't dumb.

It's a slow process. Our adults sidle gingerly into their recoveries, bit by bit becoming more willing to break through their roles and emotional shutdowns to feelings buried underneath. And with parallel gingerliness and hesitation, our kids inch their ways toward entrusting us with their emotional truth. The adults' denial systems always fight their progress; the kid's paranoia and anger always resist theirs. It's like two teams of miners, each starting from opposite sides of the mountain, hoping their two tunnels will meet somewhere in the middle.

The adult and the child both want to heal, yet they're both scared to heal. Intriguingly enough, each must let go of the same denial structure, the role. For the child, it's the shield behind which he's hidden all these years. For the adult, it's the nearest thing to a genuine identity he's ever had. Surrender by either is not lightly undertaken nor easily accomplished.

But, slowly, they edge together. The child learns he must once again trust if he wants to live, and the adult learns that to be alive he must feel.

There's a necessary context within which it all must happen. We humans may be beings of untold possibilities, capable of great accomplishment and heroism, but to repeat, we are not God. We're like rockets still on the launching pad. Once our motors are ignited, we're awesome in our power, but like it or not, somebody or something else has to hit the ignition switch before we can fire. We're back to dependency once again.

There has to be a human context for our healing. It can be a Twelve-Step program, or a therapy group, or a community of friends, or a spiritual association. But whatever it is, somebody (or bodies) has to give us a "place" of safety and unconditional acceptance where we're welcome not in spite of our brokenness but because of it. Given that gift, we can recover.

An ironic scene, enacted by client after client, occurs when I get told, "I don't know what to do. My relationship just blew up in my face. I've been fired. I've been so depressed I don't have the energy to kill myself. My cat ran away. And my best friend's deserted me." I mirror back in reply, "So your life's not working . . . ?," only to get my head snapped off with an indignant, "It is, *too!*"

By ourselves, in our denial, we simply can't accept that it's really *that* bad. Only when someone else can be more accepting of us than we can be of ourselves do we have the chance of getting through our denial and into recovery. Only when somebody will love and nurture (create) us can we love and nurture (create) ourselves; such is the dynamic of human dependency and interconnection.

The Key

Finally, I think, we've come to *the* issue of recovery, the pivot upon which all else swings, the source of joy and peace (and laughter) that alone makes embarking on this journey worthwhile at all. When all's said and done, when all the approaches to recovery have been expounded and tested, the measure of their value and effectiveness will be gauged by their ability to unchain once again the creative spirit of those victimized and enslaved by addictive dependencies. That's *the* issue, the recovery of human creativity.

Whether we speak of chemical dependency, codependency, or ACOA patterns, the ultimate tragedy wrought by these enslavements and their foundations of denial is that they insidiously, progressively smother their victims' creative, enlivening spirit. When we practice our dependencies, we make a trade: creative responsibility and freedom for security; possibility for predictability; exploration, risk, and challenge for the safely known and familiar. In short, we choose to be run, controlled, and stifled by our fears.

Concretely: One of my persisting dreams has been to write. During my drinking and using, however, and even into my recovery until I began to deal with my codependent and ACOA issues, every time I tried to write, I was continually blocked and verbally constipated. I couldn't get my thoughts from my brain, down through my arms and fingers, onto the paper. I'd try, but every word got censored, every punctuation mark got weighed against some mythical standard of literary perfection, and every sentence petered out under the weight of depressive lethargy. I gave up hope of ever being an author.

Eventually, though, in a time neither of my choosing or control, I was invited to submit a proposal for this book. I accepted, more to see if I could finally do it than anything else, and have been amazed since by how the words and ideas have flowed. More amazing yet has been the fact that it's been fun—much more play than work. My kid's had a ball, and my adult's beginning to get the full picture (for the first time, really) of what his recovery's all about. What I do today to write is show up for drill, get out of my own way (finally), and write until I get tired. My editors do their editing (very well, by the way) and nudge me on when I feel lazy; the book takes care of itself. To this perfectionistic controller, it's an unsettling experience because my "ego" has little to do with the process.

I've read and heard many a wise person say that happiness will without fail slip through our fingers if we go after it directly. They say that "it" (happiness, joy, serenity, peace, pleasure—whatever word you want) is a by-product, something that comes along naturally and easily just by doing the next indicated things in our lives. To my denial-based, addictively dependent, controllingly grandiose ego, such observations seemed so simplistic as to be ridiculous. But, as always, the opposite of everything is true, and the child shall confound the adult. In spite of myself, I'm beginning to agree with the philosophy of life I once heard Bob Earll expound, "Go through the open doors." It's so much more enjoyable than continuing to pound and kick at the doors that have been painted shut.

In fact, very few chemical dependents and codependents are not first children of alcoholic, addicted, or otherwise dysfunctional families. So, perforce, there are few chemical dependents or codependents who do not, in their recoveries, eventually have to face the issue of abusive childhoods. Whether they realize that's what they're doing—or even use the same words—the reality with which they grapple is the one I'm discussing. For to recover from any dependency means to recover one's freedom; and if "to recover freedom . . ." means anything, it must at least be that we can once again (or maybe for the first time), creatively focus in on our own lives.

Perspective

Thus the image and metaphor of the child is a near-perfect symbol for this process because childhood, is, above all else, a time of wonder, possibility, and spontaneity—the wellsprings of creativity.

The point to creativity is not the "doing" of perfect goals, perfectly achieved, but rather the "doing" of curiosity, wonder, exploration, loving, feeling, sharing, grieving, starting, and starting over again. We humans are not God; our creativity is not self-generating. We are begotten, nurtured, raised, and sustained within and through the creativity of others. But in their creativity of us, we can find the imagination and energy to be creative of ourselves and of those to whom we, in turn, give birth, nurture, and love.

As we begin our recoveries, most of us, because of the violence of our programming and the lived reinforcement of our addictive lifestyles, find ourselves fearful of, embarrassed by, and intensely distrustful of the child. Specifically, we fear the child's unbridled emotions. They're too intense, too powerful, too shamefully "inappropriate." We glue our hands to our emotional volume controls, making absolutely sure the dial never gets raised beyond "2" on a scale of "1 to 10." Addictive dependents are infamous for wild lives and extreme behaviors but, if the truth be told, when it comes to our true emotions, we're nothing short of boring in our timidity.

Creative lives are lives lived for their own sake. They do not need a chemical to give them meaning, another person to give them worth, a perfectly enacted image to give them validity. Creative lives are empowered lives, lived from the viewpoint of possibility rather than sanction. Creative lives don't get in their own way, aren't so obsessed by the need to control that they're unable to flow. Creative lives are clear-sighted, honest lives—not trapped in the fantasy of unattainable perfection, but rather so acceptingly rooted in the here and now that they can see, as Alva once described it, their connection "to the farthest star and the nearest tree."

God knows, there are few humans gifted like Michelangelo, yet there's a story about him that illustrates my point. It seems one day he was prowling some back alley in Florence when he stumbled on an enormous block of marble. Some other sculptor had thrown it away because of a flaw running through its length. Michelangelo, too, saw the flaw, but he saw it as the flowing curve of the body of his masterpiece "David." The flaw in the marble became the source of his creation.

So, in conclusion, just as Michelangelo had to surrender to and embrace the brokenness of the marble, we need to face, accept, surrender to, and even embrace the flaws of our dependently broken lives. Those flaws may not be the sources of creativity we'd have chosen for ourselves if we were God, but they are the ones we've been given. They are not to be denied or ignored, otherwise we'll miss what little chance we have left to make of ourselves, if not masterpieces, at least passable works of art.

And, last of all, when you analyze it, genuine laughter and humor always flow from the pratfall, the incongruous, the flaw, the unexpected. Speaking for myself, I've had enough fakery, perfection, and seriousness. I'm not choosy. After too many years of no laughter at all, I'll take it today when and where I can get it. If that means reuniting with my child, well . . .

Whoopee!

Chapter 13

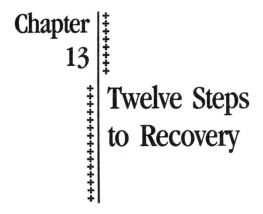

Twelve Steps to Recovery

Learning How to Live Once Again

This chapter introduces our discussion of the recovery process embodied in Twelve-Step programs. As I begin it, I find myself coming full circle to the first days of my own recovery, and, as well, contending with much the same sort of resistance I then faced. I'm having to struggle for my words, and the pen feels awkward in my hand.

Let me share with you what happened back then, over nine years ago.

I felt insulted at my first AA meeting when I saw my marching orders hanging there on the wall, unframed and gritty from the smoke of countless cigarettes. What an obnoxious list of quaintly worded "do's and don'ts":

We:

1. Admitted we were powerless over alcohol—that our lives had become unmanageable.

2. Came to believe that a Power greater than ourselves could restore us to sanity.

3. Made a decision to turn our will and our lives over to the care of God *as we understood Him.*

4. Made a searching and fearless moral inventory of ourselves.

5. Admitted to God, to ourselves, and to another human being the exact nature of our wrongs.

6. Were entirely ready to have God remove all these defects of character.

7. Humbly asked Him to remove our shortcomings.

8. Made a list of all persons we had harmed, and became willing to make amends to them all.

9. Made direct amends to such people whenever possible, except when to do so would injure them or others.

10. Continued to take personal inventory and when we were wrong promptly admitted it.

11. Sought through prayer and meditation to improve our conscious contact with God *as we understood Him,* praying only for knowledge of His will for us and the power to carry that out.

12. Having had a spiritual awakening as the result of these steps, we tried to carry this message to alcoholics, and to practice these principles in all our affairs.[1]

Puhleeze! I was an adult. I had the years, the degrees, the ordination, and the experience to prove it. I'd spent my life getting sophisticated, trying to rid myself of the rigid oversimplifications—the black-and-white do's and don'ts—of my childhood. These "Steps" stank of the pietisms of my past. In spite of the strength of my desire to stop hurting, I almost walked away from that first meeting when I read them.

That's a summary of my conscious thoughts at the time—my understanding. But, as usual, my understanding was a cover-up, a smoke

[1]Alcoholics Anonymous World Services, *Alcoholics Anonymous* (New York: AA World Services, 1976), pp. 59, 60.

screen for what was really going on, and what continues to go on even today. Truth was, I was plain, bloody *scared* by that drab list of guidelines for life.

My fear presents an ongoing message to me—and also, perhaps, to you—for I find that my reaction to the Steps is anything but unique. It's a message that needs airing as we start digging into this particular approach to recovery.

My fear was (is) about two things. The first says more about my grandiosity than anything else: I was scared of being laughed at if any of my highly educated and intelligent friends found out I was taking these inelegantly phrased commandments seriously. (I told you earlier: The more desperate my straits, the more snobbish I get.) It's the second point to the fear message, however, which is more to the point of this chapter.

Yesterday morning I sat in a restaurant with my brother. He's the editor of Seattle's *Freedom Socialist* newspaper and a leader among left-wing social activists in this area—for me, not a comfortable person with whom to converse. He's intense, convinced, and committed to his beliefs. What's more, he's intelligent and, because of his party's discipline, has learned to channel his anger's passion. He's studied and researched his issues; he's made of himself an excellent investigative reporter and good writer.

Bob is a graduate of the streets, matriculated in the social maelstrom of the sixties and seventies, and rooted in the same dysfunctional family from which I sprang. He's done his recovery, and I've done mine. The structures and philosophies that guide us couldn't be more different, yet the results—us, as we are today—are amazingly similar, uncomfortably similar. (Independent of each other, we've even each ended up smoking the same obscure brand of cigarettes.)

Until recently, we got along together as you might expect a Hero and a Scapegoat would—miserably. Over the past couple of years, though, that's started to change. I think we're finding we enjoy and respect each other—when he doesn't proselytize me and I don't big-brother him. I'm probably as skeptical of his socialism as he is of my Twelve Steps, yet neither of us can deny what the other's program has done for him. We've both become interesting, inquiring, challenging, vital, irascible, nonconforming men. We'll each probably always be more at home on society's fringes than in the mainstream, but I doubt that either of us could ever let the rest of the world pass him by unnoticed. In short, we've become a couple of creative and alive human beings. Not too bad for two men who've known addiction, insanity, and despair.

In sum, I guess you wouldn't be far off the mark to call either of us a "radical." Neither of us chose to end up that way, but the individual courses of our lives left us little alternative. How the experiences of Bob's life and their interplay with *Freedom Socialist* philosophy have resulted in his radicalism is Bob's to interpret. I can tell you about my radicalism, though, and I have no doubt today that I am who I am because of my lived response to the challenge of the Twelve-Step program.

What's more, based on my observation of my compatriots in recovery—again, based on results—I'd bet my last dollar that the values involved in this approach to recovery will radicalize anyone—including you—who takes them seriously.

In saying that, I'm not implying that you'll end up with political viewpoints or social philosophies identical to mine (or my brother's) if you embrace the Twelve-Step belief system. I'm not suggesting that you would (or should) end up thinking like I do, either. What's at stake here is far deeper than mere politics, or even philosophy.

What I do assert is that *anyone who takes recovery seriously has to develop a willingness to question everything . . . every thing.*

That requirement scared me nine years ago, and it continues to scare me today. If you find yourself resisting this discussion, if you feel your hackles rising as you read the Twelve Steps and read these pages, you are probably experiencing the same sort of fear I discovered. Lest the fear overtake you, lest you throw the book down in disgust, share in a couple of stories about my first (and deepest) dependency to help clarify where I'm going with this.

The last thing my mother would wish would be for me to be "tied to her apron strings." In fact, I have an early memory of being extremely angry at her when she wouldn't protect me from a gang of snowball-throwing bullies. I was in kindergarten in Juneau, Alaska, and Mom taught third grade in the same school. Inevitably, she would still have work to do beyond the time my class was over, and so I usually walked home by myself, a distance of seven or eight blocks. One day during the winter, a group of older boys was blocking the street, pelting younger kids (like me) with snowballs if we tried to pass. Being as uncomfortable with pain then as I am now, I decided to wait for Mom: I'd walk that gauntlet with her. They wouldn't dare throw snowballs at the teacher, and so I wouldn't get hit. Good plan. Well, Mom came along a few minutes later as expected, but she told me I'd have to handle this challenge by myself, that I couldn't use her to hide behind, and she went on without me.

I made it home somehow, but I was one pissed little kid when I got there. For all of Mom's determination that I grow up to be self-reliant, by the time I'd entered kindergarten it was already too late—something had already happened over which both she and I were powerless, and that had set in place the fundamental theme for my whole life.

What Happened

As I related in Chapter 12, my father died when I was four months old. Mother hasn't talked about his death often over the years, but when she has, it's been clear that her shock and pain were still very much alive.

When tragedy like that strikes a family, it's suddenly emotional-survival time. We humans instinctively grab onto lifelines; we've got no choice. Because we're in shock and depression, especially if our love has been deep, we can feel as though our lives no longer have purpose or meaning. Unconsciously, we reach out to those around us because it seems only they can give us the strength to go on. We hold on to them with an almost superhuman grip.

If the others we reach out to are adults, there's not only no harm in our neediness for their support, we pay them a compliment. If we reach out to depend on children, though, it's a different story.

We were isolated in tiny Platinum, Alaska, when my father died, edged up against the Bering Sea, a thousand miles from nowhere. I'm sure that other people in the camp tried to be of help, but I'm equally certain Mom could do little but hold on to me as we waited for the bush plane, as my daddy's body was loaded onto the plane, as we flew back to Anchorage sitting close beside his casket. What I became—what any infant in like circumstances becomes—was my mother's entire reason for "going on" . . . for a while, anyway. That's not what she wanted, or intended, but it's what happened.

The way any child hears and comprehends that kind of situation is as a *bargain*. Because a baby is a totally dependent entity, no matter what the adult intends, the infant hears, "I'll make you my reason for living . . . *If* you make me your reason for living." The earlier in the child's life the bargain is struck, the deeper and more central it becomes to his sense of himself; the deeper and more central his resulting dependency; the less able he is to grasp *in his guts* that his life needs to be lived for its own sake.

The bargain is impossibly contradictory. It bestows attention, specialness, almost a sense of omnipotence as nothing else could, for it makes the child responsible for the parent's life. Yet, it makes the child believe its life has no meaning or worth apart from the parent. It's a trap. I can only be totally special if I am totally dependent.

Around such dependency has been the core struggle of my life. God knows there've been people near me throughout the years to help me confront it—my mother, Archbishop Hunthausen, Alva, for example. But, God also knows, its grip has been total and unyielding. And in that dependency I see the roots of my ACOA issues, my codependency, and (pay attention, troops) the emotional foundations of my chemical dependency as well.

My friends and benefactors fought against it and (because they told me to, and I must do what they tell me to do, after all) I fought against it. There, in our fight, is the stark skeleton of my denial: Because I was so dependent, I would become strong, heroic, adult, self-reliant . . . independent.

There's nobody to blame in this story, no good guys and bad guys, only the twisted irony of life and the persistent reality of bad things happening to good people. My life had been designed to work for everyone else but me . . . no matter how much others wanted it to work for me.

That's why I was scared when I first read the Twelve Steps. Intuitively, at some deep and inarticulate level and despite my toxicity at the time, I knew those dozen sentences challenged me as never before to face my awesomely empty sense of "me." The Steps asked of me that I come to know—of myself, about myself, for myself—that the opposite of everything was true.

So I resisted their message, and I resist it still today. Over the years, I've watched newcomer after newcomer come to the Program and go through much the same reaction. Early recovery seems to be something most of us do with much kicking and screaming. The Twelve Steps demand of us to become radical in the Latin sense of the word, "reaching to the roots." The roots of addictive dependencies, though, are precisely what denial is designed and developed to disguise. I did not relish the assignment; I still don't. I fought it, and still do. If you are touched by addictive dependency and are about to face the challenge of recovery, I predict you'll resist just as much, fight just as hard. It may be one of the necessary ironies that "we know nothing until we know nothing," but I've yet to find anyone who delights in the exploration of that emptiness.

Because all of this is so horribly serious, let's lighten things up a little for a moment.

Last Christmas my partner, Tom Wojtowick, gave me a book by a local author, Robert Fulghum. It's called *All I Really Need to Know I Learned in Kindergarten*. The whole book's a delight, but the part that struck me hardest was the list of directions on the back of its dustcover:
This:

Share everything.

Play fair.

Don't hit people.

Put things back where you found them.

Clean up your own mess.

Don't take things that aren't yours.

Say you're sorry when you hurt somebody.

Wash your hands before you eat.

Flush.

Warm cookies and cold milk are good for you.

Live a balanced life—learn some and think some and draw and paint and sing and dance and play and work every day some.

Take a nap every afternoon.

When you go out into the world, watch out for traffic, hold hands and stick together.

Be aware of wonder.[2]

I think if Alva or some other old-timer had handed me that list instead of the Twelve Steps, and told me that it spoke to the heart of what recovery's about, I might have been far more willing to follow directions. Fulghum's words are witty and self-evidently true.

They're no less radical, actually, than the Twelve Steps, but they have about them the graceful glee of childhood. And, indeed, if all the stuff I've said about "the child" has any validity, the only way to sneak out from under the crushing load of addictive dependency and its denial is via the playground.

Children have a way of cutting through the resistance of even the most stubborn adult. If we are ever to recover the promise and joy of our lives, we have to let the children inside cut through the stubborn defenses and armors we adults have cloaked ourselves in. If we *really* want to grow up, our kids have got to be let out to do the most radical thing of all—play!

[2]Robert Fulghum, *All I Really Need to Know I Learned in Kindergarten* (New York: Villard Books, 1988).

Chapter 14

Showing Up for Drill

Recovery Happens "One Day at a Time"

Twenty-two years ago, after my ordination, one of my duties in my first parish was taking communion to people shut in because of illness or advanced age. One of the senior citizens, a sharp-tongued, sharp-witted old lady, New York–Irish in origin, lived with her daughter and son-in-law. Her daughter, equally as sharp in wit and tongue and equally as New York–Irish, became a friend and some-time drinking buddy at parish parties. She had a background in social work, as did I, and we found ourselves working together on the board of the local drop-in center for drug-affected teenagers, Heads Up.

Twelve years later, at my second AA meeting, I found myself sitting across the table from Trish, not knowing whether to blush or return the smile she grinned at me. Since then our friendship, as well as our professional partnership, has renewed itself. She doubles with Alva as one of my sponsors, and together we cofacilitate a women's recovery group on Tuesday nights.

For all of the tragedy of Trish's drinking career (a broken marriage, loss of her children, and time on Skid Road), her recovery has been even more dramatic. She's reestablished a deep connection with her now-grown children; she has a new relationship founded on the mutual recoveries of herself and her partner;

once again she's doing therapy—to her delight and her clients' benefit.

Best of all, from my personal view, her wit and tongue have mellowed with wisdom and compassion while losing none of their aim. Her passion for justice has had its brittle edge smoothed by a wonderful—and sometimes wacky—sense of humor.

She's another redhead. Her Queens accent complements her straightforward, extroverted style. Like Tom, she positively delights in stomping on ground angels would fear to tread. Like Alva, she has an infallible nose for "bullshit," and an unhesitating urge to confront it; nobody, but nobody, ever doubts where he or she stands with Trish. Along with Tom and Alva, she's been the third member of the triumvirate that's been my innermost core of support during recovery. They deserve no blame for my warts, and much, much credit for what remains.

Like most of us, Trish can get restive under recovery's discipline, and when she gets exasperated, frustrated, or bored, she's not mute about it. Unlike most of us, her reactions are as straightforward and "unedited" as those of a mouthy and precocious child. But whether things are rough or smooth, she's got one saying that's become her program trademark and personal mantra: "Ya gotta show up for drill."

Robert Fulghum, meet Trish D., meet Alva L., meet the Twelve Steps. You each use your own unique style to speak the same truths.

Fulghum is warm and witty:

> When you go out into the world, watch out for traffic,
> hold hands and stick together;

Trish and Alva give wry imperatives:
> Show up for drill! (Trish)

> Go to meetings; don't drink and use between meetings;
> work the steps; get a sponsor; and follow directions;
> which are . . . (Alva)

The Twelve Steps are point-by-point explicit. Here are the first three:

We:

1. Admitted we were powerless over alcohol—that our lives had become unmanageable;

2. Came to believe that a Power greater than ourselves could restore us to sanity;

3. Made a decision to turn our will and our lives over to the care of God *as we understood Him.*

Leading the Horse to Water

Before you roll your eyes and conclude I'm totally off my gourd, let me explain. Remember: The focus of all we've discussed is the addictive dependent's belief system of denial. That denial—expressing itself through the chemical dependent's drug usage, the codependent's emotionally anesthetizing depression, and the ACOA's habitual hibernation behind a role—cuts us off from the rest of the world. Generally, the erosion is slow, but it's nonetheless inevitable and unrelenting. The deeper we progress into our diseases, the more disconnected we become. In recovery, then, the key is reconnection.

If reconnection is to be genuine, though, not just another example of our frantic need to be in control, it needs to be on reality's terms, not ours.

Nice general principles; let's get specific. My chemical dependency, codependency, and ACOA patterns all play variations on the same theme: They're sicknesses that tell me I'm not sick. The more I practice them, the more I believe their message—in spite of the progressive disintegration of my life and world.

Only when I finally hit bottom did my pain finally break through my denial enough to hit me with the truth. No matter how anyone else saw me or judged me, *my truth* was that I was a drunken, emotionally dependent, perpetually defensive, isolated wreck well on his way to lonely, slow-motion self-destruction. That's what doing it my way had got me. What's worse, by the time I got to my bottom, I literally didn't know how to do my life otherwise. I was locked in. I couldn't trust myself to do and live other than I'd been doing and living. That was the hard, cold, naked fact.

So there was no alternative: To live, I had to choose to trust. I had to consult people who knew how to do what I no longer knew how to do—and follow their directions, which boiled down to: "Join us; face—accept—your truth; trust." They offered me community, confrontation, and compassionate support. It didn't go down easily. I was a priest, after all, by definition a community builder, a confronter of the denial and brokenness of others, and a bestower of forgiving healing and compassion. I mean, I wasn't a *child,* for God's sake!

I told them I had a "problem" with alcohol; *they* told me I was an alcoholic who couldn't not drink. *I* told them that in spite of my problems, I was in control; *they* told me that based on results, I was insane. *I* told them I needed nobody; *they* told me being sufficient unto myself got me where I was, and that my alternatives were either accept what they offered or get a refund on my misery and pain. My head refused to track with their logic, but my gut kept saying I had no other choice. So, to stop hurting, I decided to shelve intellect and understanding for the time being and just do what they told me to do. In a nutshell, that's the story of my first two to two-and-a-half years of sobriety: doing what I was told to do, not because I agreed, but because I had no other choice. Petulantly, often unenthusiastically, I simply kept showing up for drill.

And then a funny thing happened. Somewhere in my third year, I woke up to realize that "their" Program worked, because my life had started to work for the first time—for me. "Their" Program hád become *my* Program. I didn't know it at the time, but I had yet to confront my codependent and ACOA issues. Nevertheless, I now had the one thing I'd never before had . . . hope.

At that point, I became aware that I'd done the basics of the first three steps of the Program. I had no doubts left about my powerlessness over alcohol or the unmanageability of my life. *What had been* stood out all too dramatically against *what now was.*

My insanity had made itself obvious—the kind of insanity the Program defines as "doing the same thing over and over again while expecting different results." Well, I'd done the same thing again and again (making life, people, and things go *my* way), and the results had always been the same. My life always worked for them, but not for me. But now, that had begun to change. Left to my own devices, that change might never have occurred. By putting myself in their hands, showing up for drill, and following their directions, my own natural order was able to surface for the first time. It was like (perhaps more than just "like") being a kid again.

Last of all, there was trust. By the time I got to bottom, I was no longer sure of a God for me—for others, maybe, but not for me. Since I was in denial about my dependencies, whatever conscious reasons I had for that absence of faith were basically bullshit, but the doubt itself was real. With today's clarity, I can see that my chemicals, upon which I was dependent, had become my "Higher Power." Any intellectual reasons I employed to argue God's existence or lack thereof were nothing more than denial, cover-ups for my real belief: "There is no god but chemistry."

First Things First

Sobriety and the Program haven't proved that there is a God, or, more specifically, that there is a God for me. But they've told me something more obvious. They teach me I'm human, that I'm chemically dependent, that I'm emotionally dependent, that I'm an ACOA. By definition, any of the above renders me insufficient unto myself. Put them all together in a quadruple whammy, and even I can't argue myself out of the conclusion. Dependent people do dependent things—that is, they depend. They cannot do otherwise. I've no choice about being dependent, and neither does any other human being. I can choose to go into my depending—my neediness—kicking and screaming, or gracefully and easily, but as surely as death and taxes will come, I *will* go.

From what I can see, there's nobody not in the same boat. Even the power brokers of our world need people and things over which they can exert their domination—just to be powerful. Even the weakest and most subject need air to breathe, food to eat, and masters to serve—in contrast to whom they find their servility—just to be weak. Relational interdependence is the bedrock, inescapable fact of human existence. That's obvious today, even if nothing else is. I've been able to discover it only because I showed up for drill—again and again—when it made sense and when it didn't—and found there was always someone there where once there had been nothing.

So now . . . kids . . . the fun begins. We can and do argue God's existence. But (I suspect) whatever individual and social conclusions we come to as a result of those arguments, they're irrelevant in the last analysis. These days I'm led to look on theological disputations and religious wars with much suspicion; all too often, they have about themselves the "smell" of denial. I may be cynical but, when I hear of such wars of words and blood, I tend to hear the sideways exploding rage of human beings denying their interdependency, their connectedness, and the confusing pain those unavoidable bondings often cause. Denial kills.

So, today, I still don't know if I believe in God; when it comes to divinity, all I know is that I don't know. What I do know is that I need, I depend; and that I can battle against my need and dependency or I can accept them in peace; and that when I battle, I hurt. Thus, I'm caught in a paradox: The evidence of my past says there's no reason to trust; the evidence of my today says that trust alone can work; *and both those propositions are true.* (Remember how impossible it was to figure out the grown-ups in your childhood? Welcome back to kindergarten.)

Therefore—would I rather be right or would I rather be happy? I've no doubt about my answer to that question, so today I choose to quit the game of disputing God's existence, and instead choose to trust. On some days that trust is placed in a "Higher Power" who sometimes get addressed as "Lord" or at other times (as Trish says) gets called "Ralph." On other days, my trust sees no further than my friends and community in recovery. On some other days, finally, my trust is nothing more than a willingness to be *willing* to trust, a willingness to keep showing up for drill. Whatever, I keep choosing to trust because, without trust, I've no hope.

That's a highly personalized, sketchy outline of my wrestlings with the first three Steps of the Twelve-Step program. Take what you need, leave the rest. I doubt, though, that anyone in recovery would deny that these are the issues. My words and ways of reflecting about it all may not be yours—nor do they have to be—but trust, confusion, bewilderment, anger, finding a new Higher Power, and reconnecting are what we all are involved with in our recoveries.

Unless You Become As Little Children . . .

Let's lay aside this adult palaver and get back to Mr. Fulghum's kindergarten. *"When you go out into the world, watch out for traffic, hold hands and stick together."* Any kid would intuitively know that's how to sum up all the stuff I've been talking about in this chapter. When it comes to the world and to traffic, kids usually know that they're little, and that it feels good and secure to holds hands with somebody else as the cars go zooming by.

I'm no child psychologist, but I'll bet my next warm cookie that what most kids want most of the time is to be kids. All other things being equal (which they never are), kids don't worry about growing up. That's just "something that happens." Take potty training, for instance. We adults worry about it, and work at it, and get frustrated—and kids develop neuroses because of our worry and frustration. The fact of the matter is that nine times out of ten, as babies' sphincters develop in the due course of time, the kids will become potty trained automatically, all by themselves.

Recovery's like that. It happens, almost automatically—*if we get out of the way.* The body will detoxify at *its* own pace, in *its* own time; feelings will surface less and less distorted, in *their* own time; relationships will grow and reconnect themselves, at *their* own pace. Our job, like that of kids crossing the street, is to dodge the traffic and hold on to one another. Showing up for drill—every day—has kept me out of the traffic.

Broaden out the discussion: The process fits for codependent and ACOAs as well. Among others, Carl Rogers, (the developer of "person-centered" therapy) continually pointed out how the human organism has an inner impulse or dynamic that impels it to heal and grow. If we look at codependent and ACOA programming as blocks to growth—as impedances to our development resulting from neglect and trauma—the recovery process for these forms of addictive dependency runs exactly parallel to that for chemical dependency.

Those of us caught in codependent and ACOA patterns are stuck in the same sort of repetitive cycle as chemical dependents—hemmed in by our denial systems just like a wagon train surrounded by Indians. We're trapped in the illusion that our defenses give us control over our lives, that our survival roles render us impervious to the normal connections and dependencies of life. In short, we forgo our growth in an all-too-painful real world for the anesthesia of a prolonged fantasy.

Given the families and relationships in which codependents and children of alcoholics find themselves, it's hard to criticize their headlong, total, compulsive flight into fantasy. But those flights have become habitual, an addictive way of life. Ultimately we—like chemical dependents—have to face the same stark dilemma: Grow up or die. And if we choose the path of growth, we will find ourselves working through the issues posed by the first three Steps of the Twelve-Step programs. We shall have to face and accept the truth of our dependencies. We shall have to recognize that the flight that once gave us survival now makes us insane. We shall have to choose to trust. And because these actions are so threatening to the belief system we've obeyed for so many years, the only course that will keep us on track is to follow whatever version of these three first Steps works for us . . . and just continue to show up for drill.

Perspective

When the fire bell sounds, first-graders would rather run for their lives into the playground and the streets in an automatic "flight for survival." It's perfectly natural that they should "believe" that running as fast as you can is the best choice.

But firemen and teachers could die in a burning building while searching for an unaccounted-for child. Children blindly running from real or imagined infernos could get run over by passing trucks. That's why there are fire drills, because children don't "understand" any further than "I don't want to die," or "It's an emergency! Run, don't walk!"

In their guts, it doesn't make any sense to walk calmly out of a burning schoolhouse. Children have to trust their teachers' guidance, because what the children don't know could kill them.

That's what the drills are for: molding lifesaving behavior into habit.

Chapter 15

Once Upon a Time . . .

"Just the Facts, Ma'am . . . Just the Facts"

I heard a story about Sigmund Freud that may or may not be true—but that should be if it isn't. Seems he's supposed to have told some of his followers that when a client could come into his office and spend the whole session simply telling his story with no interruptions, no interpretations, and no judgments, he was ready to leave therapy. He would be in touch with his true self.

The other night a client shared with me a parable he'd heard at a Native American sweat ceremony. It has much the same point as the Freud story. Over the years, I've heard several different editions of the parable, but this one was especially charming:

Many, many years ago, the tribe was in great danger and the leaders did not know what to do. So they went to the wise old shaman of the tribe. But he, too, was afraid, for he had no answers for the People's fear. He decided, therefore, to take his three helpers and go on a medicine quest to implore the Great Spirit for guidance.

The four of them went out into the wilderness and the three helpers kept attendance on the old man as he fell into a trance. The Great Spirit came upon him in his trance, and when he awoke, he had knowledge of a sacred place whither he had to go to pray for the People, and he knew as well a sacred dance to dance there, and a sacred song to sing. He went there with his three young helpers, and he prayed and he danced and he sang there, and the People were saved.

Years later, shortly before the last of his helpers—now an old man himself—breathed his last, the People were once again in great danger. As before, the leaders came to the shaman for guidance. And he said, "I do not remember the place, but I do remember the dance and the song." So he danced the dance and sang the song, and the People were saved.

After that, when his helper was aged, the same thing happened, and the leaders came once more for help. This old man said, "I do not remember the place or the dance, but I do remember the song." So he sang the song, and the People were saved.

Then it was the time of the last of the great shamans. One final time the People were in danger, and the leaders sought the wise elder's aid. His memory was dimmed by his years, and so he said, "I do not remember the place, or the dance, or the song; but I do remember the story." So he told the story—and the People were saved.

Our stories heal. All the great spiritual traditions know that. That's why Christians have the "memorial" of the Eucharist; why Jews remember Passover; why Islam reveres the history of the Prophet. There's something in the telling of a story that cuts through the befogging rationalizations of our minds to touch our hearts. Thus, the magic of the theater and stage.

By definition, addictive dependencies cut us off from our roots and isolate us from being in touch with our stories. Whether the isolating agent is chemicals, or depression, or the numbing buffer of an ACOA role, it's always rooted in a belief system of denial, and *that* cuts us off from our own truth.

In the initial stage of recovery, prodded on by the pain of hitting bottom, we get in contact with the fundamental statement of our truth—that we *are* chemically addicted, that we *are* codependent, that we *are* ACOA. But discovering that fundamental truth, even surrendering to and accepting it, is usually not enough. Eventually, the pain of the bottom passes, and the patterns of our former lifestyles begin to reassert themselves, even in spite of the communities of support we've gathered about ourselves.

The one exercise that seems able to fix us in our course of recovery is getting in touch, in detail, with our full story, and then sharing it. When I was in treatment, the single most beneficial assignment they gave me was to write an autobiography. I worked on it for over four weeks, and eventually came up with forty-five or so single-spaced sheets of paper.

Like everyone in early sobriety, I was chemically toxic at the time, and my emotions were consequently numbed and distorted. Nevertheless, as I wrote down the facts of my story, I laughed and I cried, and I came to know my truth. I've seen my experience duplicated time and time again by others as they go through their recoveries.

AA has a tradition of "speakers' meetings," wherein various individuals get up and share their stories. Having been on both the giving and receiving end of such meetings, I can testify that whatever the audience learns from the speaker's "experience, strength, and hope," the one doing the talking gains immeasurably more. Nothing makes the happenings and behaviors of my life more real to me than hearing my own voice tell of them. Storytelling works.

Bobbing and Weaving

No step in the recovery process meets stronger resistance. When you ask people in recovery to share their stories, you can count on running headlong into forgetfulness, evasion, partial truths, blackouts, eruptions of "uproar" in other areas of life, perhaps even a return to drinking and using—in a word, any and every imaginable kind of resistance. It's as if the addictive part of us knows only too well that more than anything else, the telling of our stories sounds its death knell.

The resistance gets almost comic at times. I had one client who simply snapped into a deep sleep any time I tried to question her about the specifics of her chemical abuse or her childhood. I knew what she was doing; she knew what she was doing; yet she still did it. It literally took her nine months and forty-eight naps to tell me her story (and she was only twenty-four years old!).

That resistance is, in fact, a living symposium on denial and its power. When people come into recovery, they do so because they have to and they want to. So, on a conscious level, they do not want to resist the process; yet they do.

For us addictive dependents, our resistance's number-one ally is shame, guilt. We may not remember much of what we did as we practiced our dependencies, but we're damned sure that, whatever it may have been, it was bad, dirty, ugly, dishonorable, dishonest, criminal, and altogether repugnant. We may be accepting and compassionate toward others caught in the same patterns and pressures as we, but toward ourselves, we can only be ashamed and judgmental. Since much of what we did was abusive and destructive (addicted people do addicted things, after all), our shame and guilt make sense.

Thus, I don't know one of us—given his druthers—who wouldn't "let sleeping dogs lie." "Why reopen old wounds and dig up the past?" "I want to get on with my life, not get stuck in the past!" "It's just an exercise in self-flagellation!"

Any way you cut it, all our resistance adds up to one thing: We're afraid of our pasts, we're afraid of ourselves. You see, telling our stories brings us face-to-face once again with our powerlessness . . . and our victimization.

But, as we've discussed previously, there's also a payoff to staying in our fear and shame. If we're *that* guilty, then we must be *that* big, *that* powerful, *that* important. So, besides being just plain scared to look once again at our pasts, we're actually invested in keeping the pages of our personal histories closed. Aggrandizing one's "ego" by being *that* ashamed and *that* guilty may seem like a masochistic way to assert one's specialness—but, at this most primitive level of survival, anything's better than nothing.

Powerless Once Again

But if we do reexamine and retell our pasts, eventually we're going to collide with the truth that there's not one of us who ever sat down at age five or six or seven to deliberately choose to become a chemical dependent, a codependent, or an ACOA. Once we face that truth, we will also have to face the twin facts that we are powerless and that we are genuinely victims. Those of us who are chemically dependent must face that we're powerless before the addictive potency of our substances; they victimize us. Those of us who are codependent must face that we're powerless before the addictive potency of our relational programming; it victimizes us. And those of us who are ACOA must face that we're powerless over the potency of the abuse of our childhoods and the defensive roles we had to devise for survival; they victimized us.

Once we truly confront all those truths, once we really *know* them, we can and shall grieve. We'll see the decisions we had to make, we'll get in touch with the loneliness of choosing when nothing made sense, we'll go through the feelings we need to process (the feelings against which we've anesthetized ourselves all these years), and then we may have a chance of getting on with our lives.

But getting on with our lives implies becoming responsible for ourselves, becoming creative, becoming self-generating. That's new ground for us, new and frightening ground. The old ways may have hurt, but they were familiar—we knew the steps to their dance. At age forty it was not comfortable when I finally, seriously faced the question, "What do I want to be when I grow up?"

No wonder, therefore, our resistance to telling our stories. Our guts seem to know intuitively where it will lead, and they rebel. Wouldn't *you*, if someone said you had to be parachuted at midnight into a foreign land, with no knowledge of the language or the culture, with orders that you were supposed to build a totally new identity and life since there was next to no chance you could ever return to who and what you once were? That's the implied result (and threat) of this storytelling process.

Just Do It

There're many ways storytelling can happen. A treatment center might have us write autobiographies. Therapists might invite us to sit or lie down on the couch, and then bid us tell them who we are "from the beginning." A friend might ask, "What happened?" The Twelve-Step programs tell us to do a "Fourth and Fifth Step," share a moral inventory of our life with someone else.

Whatever the context for relating our stories, I'm convinced this kind of self-sharing is a completely necessary aspect of recovery. It accomplishes three things that are at the very core of healing: 1. it gives us an in-depth, detailed diagnosis of our brokenness and makes us discover just how bad our lives were; 2. it forces us to get in touch with ourselves by breaking through our denial; and 3. it propels us out of our isolation, demanding of us to choose to share our truth with another.

Just telling our stories does not guarantee we will never again use our chemicals or regress into our addictive emotional patterns. But it does ensure that if we do slip or regress, we'll know 1. *what* we're doing, and 2. that our defensive shields of denial will never again be so impenetrable or so powerful.

The last benefit of this storytelling process is that once we discover the concrete, detailed truth about ourselves, we can become ready and willing to change.

For example, as I progressed in my drinking, my alcoholism corroded away any sense of hope or optimism I had about life and human relationships. I became a despairing cynic; I saw whatever goodness and caring other people manifested as nothing more than sham, manipulation, cons, or naiveté. When I surrendered to my alcoholism, however, and came to an intimate, detailed knowledge of my addictive denial, I had to face up to the fact that all the rationalizations I'd spun as justification for my cynicism were meaningless. Because I am who I am, I'd constructed an elaborate intellectual structure—drawn from philosophy, theology, sociology, and psychology—to assure myself and anyone else who might be interested that this creation was as empty and absurd as I felt it to be. My "worldview" was logical, coherent, impressive; I won more than one debate with it; but, at its heart, it was nothing more than the efforts of a terrified little puppy trying to defend himself against the pain of his own hurt. It was, in AA terms, my "bullshit," my denial.

As my recovery has progressed, slowly—ever so slowly—that worldview has melted away; I've let go of it. My logic is still logical;

my thoughts are still coherent; but, today, they simply don't seem to matter anymore. Because I'm no longer invested in my defenses, because I no longer have to hold on to my denial, I find myself free to change. More precisely, all that philosophical justification and intellectual rigidity is now . . . obsolete. I just don't need it anymore.

I didn't choose to jettison this "baggage." I didn't figure up some even more potent arguments to disprove it. It evaporated like the morning mist. There've been occasions over the past several years, in fact, when I've tried to reclaim my cynicism. But somehow, maybe like a shell a crab outgrows, it no longer fits. Telling my story—as often as I've been given the opportunity—dissolved my defenses; and with my defenses gone, I've changed and grown.

Kindergarten rules enjoin, "Don't lie. Tell the truth." The Gospels claim ". . . the truth shall make [us] free." The Twelve-Step programs say we:

4. Made a searching and fearless moral inventory of ourselves.
5. Admitted to God, to ourselves, and to another human being the exact nature of our wrongs.
6. Were entirely ready to have God remove all these defects of character. . . .

Therapists bid us tell them our stories. Treatment centers have us write our autobiographies. Take your pick of which set of directions you find most congenial. Bottom line, though, the processes those different sets of words entail are one and the same. Whichever road you choose to take, at the end will be the signpost saying ". . . [A]nd so he told the story, and the People were saved."

Chapter 16

Of Kittens and Getting On with Life

Being Alive: The Biggest Deal of All

Since I've begun this book, there's been a new addition to my home. He's a little long-haired white kitten with green-gold eyes, whose low purr rumbles like a freight train. In a most unfelinelike way, he loves to lie nestled on his back in the crook of my arm to get his belly rubbed. And if I'm busy, Loki's an acceptable Dutch uncle: The kitten rolls over in ecstasy to let ninety-five pounds of dog give him a tongue-washing; then he curls up between Loki's paws to snooze. Princess's nose is out of joint at his invasion, of course, but lately I've noticed that she'll occasionally rub nostrils with him or join in a chase through the house without hissing and growling. The other day I even caught them asleep, side by side, in the same chair. He looks Russian to me, so I call him Pushkin.

He's the only extrovert in the household, which guarantees him all the attention he wants—the more, the merrier. His favorite perch—from the first moment he arrived—is on my shoulder, purring into my ear. Usually, it's an agreeably warm, shivery feeling to have him there, but he blew my dignity one day. During a therapy session, he climbed from my shoulder to the top of my head. I had to leave him there because when I began to lift him off, he started to dig in. Discretion, I decided, was the better part of valor; bald may be beautiful, but there are drawbacks. At least my client departed the session with more of a smile on his face than when he entered. Kittens really don't give a damn about one's professional image.

Life's like that: Eventually, we all discover the sad reality that it, like Pushkin, doesn't give a damn about our pretensions and images, either. Whether we deny it, or fight it, or try to ignore it, life goes on. Death happens (cryogenics notwithstanding)—and birth happens—and comes another day.

As for the rest of life, so for recovery. Once we've done our initial surrendering and stumbled through the telling of our stories, we have to get on with our lives. But that's a bigger challenge than we might at first suppose. To repeat one of our oft-spoken points, we addictive dependents—for all of our survival skills—are klutzes when it comes to living. We either forget how or never learned how in the first place.

For example, we've noted how we tend to do relationships much as Patton waged war—totally. Consequently, in our recoveries, if we run into somebody who happens to find us attractive enough to send out a hesitant opening invitation (a glance, perhaps, or a smile), we're liable to respond with a full-fledged campaign of attack, envelopment, and occupation. Or we might go to the opposite extreme and read such an invitation as a declaration of hostilities. For us, seduction implies life-and-death struggle; for the healthy, it's an invitation to play.

So we've got to go back to school—kindergarten, to be precise. We have to learn how to do life. If the first six Steps of the Twelve-Step programs can be subsumed under Fulghum's "When you go out into the world, watch out for traffic, hold hands and stick together," or Trish's "Show up for drill," the remainder of the recovery process takes longer to say and do. Compare again our two sources of wisdom:

FULGHUM	TWELVE STEPS
Share everything.	We:
Play fair.	7. Humbly asked Him to remove our shortcomings.
Don't hit People.	

Put things back where you found them.

Clean up your own mess.

Don't take things that aren't yours.

Say you're sorry when you hurt somebody.

Wash your hands before you eat!

Flush.

Warm cookies and cold milk are good for you.

Live a balanced life—learn some and think some and draw and paint and sing and dance and play and work every day some.

Take a nap every afternoon.

Be aware of wonder.

8. Made a list of all we had harmed and became willing to make amends to them.

9. Made direct amends to such people whenever possible, except when to do so would injure them or others.

10. Continued to take personal inventory and when we were wrong promptly admitted it.

11. Sought through prayer and meditation to improve our conscious contact with God *as we understood Him,* praying only for knowledge of His will and the power to carry that out.

12. Having had a spiritual awakening as the result of these steps, we tried to carry this message and to practice these principles in all our affairs.

Back to Basics

I once heard an AA speaker tell how, in a conversation with his sponsor sometime during his early recovery, he intended to divorce his wife because ". . . things had gotten so rocky between us and I didn't know if I really cared for her anymore." His sponsor listened patiently, thought for a moment, and then replied, "No, you're not! You're gonna go home and for the next year do nothing but practice good manners. At the end of the year, you can decide if you still want to leave her." Ten years later, he and his wife were still together; their marriage was better than ever.

I got a lesson along the same vein. While I was in treatment, I told my counselor I wanted to leave the priesthood. Instead, he insisted I go home, accept my assignment from the archdiocese, and practice "H-A-L-T" (an AA acronym for "Don't get too *H*ungry, too *A*ngry, too *L*onely, or too *T*ired") for at least two years. Alva agreed. So I did it—grudgingly, poutingly.

They were right. In the next four-and-a-half years, I served in two parishes. In both, I told my story and was received with loving support. Those people ministered to me—acceptingly, unconditionally. Because of them, I came to know what community and church can be at their best. I healed: My system detoxified, my bitterness dissolved, my emptiness filled. Along with my AA community, those parishes—and especially their priests—gave me back my life.

When it did come time to resign the priesthood, the reasons for my decision were totally different from those I'd held onto five years before. In all honesty, I've little doubt that I'd now be dead from my alcoholism if I'd done it my way. Decisions that important, if done in anger and negativity, backfire horribly: "What goes around comes around."

The recovery process we've outlined in the previous three chapters was about foundation building. Surrender, acceptance, learning how to trust once again, and telling one's story have but one goal: giving us the willingness to grow. That willingness, that openness to development and creativity, is the value I believe the somewhat negative wording of the Sixth and Seventh Steps is about.

For us—perhaps more than for most other people—the willingness to grow means a willingness to get out of our own way. When you consider the in-depth programming for self-destruction with which we've been imprinted, that's far more easily said than done. As Alva once told me, "There's no relationship, no situation, I can't and won't fuck up." (He's so damn delicate!)

In the concrete, I suspect that willingness translates into the construction and implementation of a habitual usage of reality checks. By now, I hope it's clear that our heads are broken; of themselves they can't be trusted. Thus we need something to balance off our natural inclination for self-corrosive chaos.

The Twelve-Step programs, in a delightful (some would say perverse) example of fighting fire with fire, constructed just the kind of community to provide that balance. There's no authority—in any common sense of the word—in the Program. Each group is governing unto itself, and its elected leaders' main job is to serve, nothing more. All you've got to do to witness organizational chaos in action is to go to an AA business meeting. There are as many interpretations of the Steps as there are members in the various programs.

And yet there is an overriding wisdom here, a collective nose for the "smell" of denial, a communal "bullshit detector" to confront each of us with reality. If we have the willingness to hear (and listen!), if we have the willingness to grow, then the message of our communities—Program, therapy, friends, church, etc.—has a good chance of guiding us in life. There *is* a collective wisdom, after all, in commands like, "Share Everything," "Play Fair," "Don't Hit People," and "Flush."

There's more involved than just a willingness to grow, however, or a willingness to check out our personal perceptions and judgments against the conscience of our groups. Fulghum's kindergarten teacher summed it up by saying, "Clean up your mess."

The Twelve Steps get more specific: ". . . (8). Made a list of all persons we had harmed and became willing to make amends to them all; (9). Made direct amends to such people wherever possible, except when to do so would injure them or others; (10). Continued to take personal inventory and when we were wrong promptly admitted it . . ." Next to the telling of our stories, there's little that we resist more in our recovery processes than cleaning up our own messes. Let's explore that resistance, for it can tell us like nothing else what's at stake.

The Truth Hurts . . . and Heals

In my own recovery, I discern two major reasons for my unwillingness to dig in and clean up my own mess. The first is akin to the reason I resisted telling my story: My mess told me—graphically and inescapably—how far down I'd gone. It hurt like hell to go mucking around in the specifics of the behavior I'd so tried to conveniently forget and suppress. It hurt to be embarrassed once again by the embarrassment I'd caused others through my drunken insensitivity and carelessness. It hurt to recall how arrogant and rigid I'd been. It hurt to remember the violations of confidence, the dishonesties, and the manipulations I'd committed. Much more, though, did it hurt to contemplate approaching those I'd injured and " 'fessing up."

Underneath my embarrassment, what was really on the line, once again, was my denial. Nothing attacks a structure of denial more than the truth spoken openly. And once that denial structure is laid bare, it becomes all the harder to return to the addicted way of life.

As I was leaving treatment, my counselor urged me, "When you get home to your parish, tell people who you are and where you've been. There's no way you'll ever be able to run down all the people you've hurt with your alcoholism, but if you start out your recovery in complete honesty, you'll know that you really are willing to make amends. Besides, if you tell them you're an alcoholic, you'll have one hell of a time if you try to get them to enable a relapse for you." It turned out to be one of the few times I've been able to use one denial system against another. I was such an ACOA Hero and people pleaser that, several times, my fear of what parishioners would think kept me from drinking. The alcoholic inside me was and is alive and powerful, but cleaning up my own mess helps keep him in remission.

The second reason I've resisted this part of the recovery process is harder to get a handle on. When I first read the Eighth and Ninth Steps, I immediately thought their purpose was to caretake and heal other people's feelings more than it was to help me. Since I was still toxic, paranoid, angry, and resentful, I could have cared less about other people's feelings at the time.

Likewise, when I finally faced the fact that I had to make my amends, I got fearful about the possible reactions of the people I had to approach. What if they wouldn't accept my apologies? What if they got angry at me? There were some who didn't even know I'd harmed them; what if I told them and they broke off our friendships as a result? Doing amends felt as though it could be the opening of a galactic can of mutant worms.

Some of my friends in recovery helped me through those fears. They showed me that the person I did my amends *for,* first and foremost, was myself. *The issue was not fixing the misdeeds of my past or the feelings of those I'd injured.* Rather, the issue was my sobriety and self-respect. In my practice of my addictive dependencies, there was nobody I'd injured and disrespected more deeply than myself. And the heart of my self-destructive disrespect and abuse was my belief system of denial. Consequently, if I were to become self-respecting and self-nurturing, I had to start knowing and telling my truth. We respect ourselves by respecting ourselves—by doing self-respecting things.

In short, before I made my amends, I had to live in my secrets and my shame. I was vulnerable, as it were, to blackmail. Once I made those amends, once I cleaned up my own mess, there weren't any secrets left; I was free.

It's not a "natural" way for me to live, but it pays off.

World Without End

Addictive dependencies are chronic. We'll discuss that in detail in the next chapter, but suffice it for the moment to say that means "they don't go away." I may be sober, but I'm still an alcoholic. I may—today—be relating in peace and acceptance, but I'm still a codependent. I may be in touch with my child, living in my truth rather than my role, but I'm still an ACOA. This stuff is too deeply imprinted in my experience and my psyche to just dry up and blow away.

My denial would love to claim I'm cured; it would be so nice to be able to forget it all, to be able to say that the nightmare's over and done with.

If I were to do that, though, it would be like the Russians forgetting the Gulag, or African-Americans forgetting slavery. We always have Stalins and Simon Legrees with us; my brokenness remains my truth. To forget invites self-destruction.

So I need to stay in touch—not as an exercise in self-flagellation but in self-preservation.

Concretely, that means I have to center and focus myself daily. It means that daily I have to reconnect with my truth, and recommit myself to my creativity and growth. It means, most of all, I have to rechoose—daily—to *trust* the process of my recovery.

Fulghum says, "Live a balanced life—learn some and think some and draw and paint and sing and dance and play and work every day some"; and: "Take a nap every afternoon." The Twelve Steps say we: ". . . (11). Sought through prayer and meditation to improve our conscious contact with God *as we understood Him,* praying only for knowledge of His will and the power to carry that out. . . ." The realities of which those differing sets of words speak are one and the same.

Normally, I have two dangerous times during my day. In the morning, when I first awake, I often open my eyes and experience what several AA speakers have described as "the Vulture" perched on my bedpost. You know . . . it's that rush of gloom that strikes just before full consciousness, intoning sepulchrally, "Have I got a day for you!" Before Loki, Princess, and Pushkin entered my life, it could be hellish—numbing my mornings and clouding my days. Today, though, their immediate demands for attention, petting, butt scratching, and all the other rituals of affection blunt its force. Nonetheless, I still have to take time to focus and open myself to a sense of gratitude for my life and this day. Never before have I been aware of what great and fragile gifts they are.

Some days I can stay in that space for a long while, and at other times it can only sustain itself for a minute or two. But if I don't give myself those moments, my day tends to go nowhere but downhill.

My second shaky time is late afternoon/early evening. In my third year of sobriety, during the time my ACOA issues surfaced in full fury, I could count on the emotional bottom dropping out of my day right at four-thirty in the afternoon. It was so predictable that I would start preparing for it at 4:20. I'd get some tissues for my tears and set the box on the table next to my favorite chair; I'd close and lock the door to my quarters and notify the parish secretary I wouldn't be taking my calls for the next two hours; and finally I'd draw the curtains, turn down the lights, and put the saddest music I could find on the tape player. (Well, if you're gonna hit bottom no matter what, you might as well go in style!) That was my ritual for close to six months. The one thing I held on to was the old AA saying, "This, too, shall pass."

Through Program, therapy, and antidepressants, those slalom rides into despair slowly faded. Nonetheless, to this day, I tend to have a two- or three-hour "dip" around suppertime.

Before recovery, the single thing above all others that made those bouts of depression so overwhelmingly devastating was my lack of hope. I had no trust, and thus I had no hope; and I had no trust because I could not hope. It was an insane and deadly vicious circle.

Yet it made a certain kind of elegant sense, too. If, through the use of my chemicals and the employment of my ACOA/codependent suppression of feelings, I was committing suicide, then the last thing I was doing was living in trust and hope of myself. And we only do to others what we're already doing to ourselves. There was no way, therefore, that I could trust or hope in my world, my God, or my brother and sister human beings.

But today—a day at a time—there is recovery, if I will but say yes to it. My inclinations and programming have not changed; nor has the world in its cruel absurdity. For all of that, however, I cannot argue that I am now sober and in recovery. That is the truth I need to touch daily. The most natural, normal, "sensical" thing in the world is for an alcoholic to drink, a codependent to codepend, and an ACOA to ACOA. But I am not doing so—and that's not for want of trying.

I don't even work too hard to keep myself out of the way of temptation. Funnily enough, however, even though I do go into bars to meet friends or just to get lost in the pleasant hum of humanity, and even though (naturally) there is alcohol all around me, I can't seem to work my way toward the bar for a Coke without a compatriot from AA running up to me "just to say hi." If I *were* embarked on a hell-bent course to get myself a cocktail, I wouldn't be able to get away with it. There's no escaping the support structure my life has arranged for me.

There is a giftedness to my life today that is the result of no virtue or strength of mine. It seems that all I have to do to keep the gift coming is to be grateful. So, for me, the heart of my almost daily focusing and centering is very simply the practice of good manners—saying "Thank you!" And I really don't care if there's a God there to hear my gratitude or not; the saying of it—*just* the saying of it—works, and is enough.

If Ya Wanna Keep It, Ya Gotta Give It Away.

At last, the Twelfth Step: ". . . Having had a spiritual awakening as the result of these steps, we tried to carry this message . . . and to practice these principles in all our affairs." When I first read this Step, I knew I'd been snookered.

First of all, it was personally insulting. I was a priest. In one of the seminaries where I served, I'd been "director of spiritual life." I'd taught courses in spirituality. They were going to give *me* a "spiritual awakening . . . ?!"

Immediately on the heels of the feeling of being insulted came an even more repugnant feeling of being trapped. I knew I had no place else to go. Insulted or not, if I wanted to stop hurting, I had to do what I was told—and they were using a phrase like ". . . *all* of our affairs." They were talking about *the rest of my life*. My gut sank, and my mind muttered, "Oh shit!" I may have been toxic, but I still had enough insight left to see the obvious.

Over the ensuing years, I've mellowed . . . somewhat. I've begun to learn that this step—like all the rest—is something I do but I don't do. If I am living in my recovery, the Twelfth Step happens in my life; if I am not—to the extent I am not, to the extent I am in my denial—it does not.

The hackle-raising buzzwords in this step are ". . . spiritual awakening." To people like me (arrogant), to committed agnostics and atheists (principled), and to graduates of the streets and abusive families (despairing cynics), "spiritual awakening" implies God, religion, and some pietistic parody of the American Way. It's a hell of a thing to be hit with on your first day of sobriety.

My sponsor was practical; he said, "Forget about Twelve, you're hardly into One." He had a very Alva look on his face and sound in his voice; so I did what he said. Acceptance and powerlessness were more than enough to occupy me for the next two to two-and-a-half years. After that came codependency and ACOA, so I doubt that it was much sooner than six years into recovery that I began to take a really serious look at Step Twelve. When it did surface for consideration, I found that the Twelfth Step had been happening in my life—all by and of itself.

Perspective

There's a saying in meetings that AA (read as well: Al-Anon, OA, ACOA, etc.) has to be ". . . a program of attraction, not of persuasion." That's the essence of the Twelfth Step: if we get sober and recover, almost in spite of ourselves we become attractive human beings. And if we become attractive in our recoveries, we are carrying the message and practicing the principles.

The most bewildering thing in my life today is that, if I just tell my truth, I have clients, and an income, and opportunity after opportunity. I—a drunk, codependent ACOA—get paid to be myself. In the shamed, guilt-ridden, finely honed logic of my denial system, that fact makes absolutely no sense. Nor have I discovered that it makes sense to the denial systems of Alva, Tom, Trish, or any other person in recovery I know. Nonetheless, it *is* what happens.

You see, the essence of what AA's Twelfth Step talks about, the guts underlying phrases like *spiritual awakening* and *practicing these principles,* is nothing more than the almost automatic result of a life lived creatively, responsively, freely. Fulghum sums it up well in his last aphorism: "Be aware of wonder."

Alva told me a delightful story that illustrates my point. One morning he was due in court at 9:00 A.M. for an important trial. He lives on Lake Sawyer, about thirty miles from Auburn, Washington, where his practice is located. The lake, besides being a gorgeous reflecting pool for Mount Rainier, is a stopover for Canadian geese during their annual migrations. On this particular morning, he was rushing to leave when a flight of the honkers swooped in right in front of his house. Alva was so taken by their beauty that he dropped his briefcase, grabbed some cracked corn, and ran down to the water's edge to feed them. Understandably, the judge, the client, and the prosecuting attorney were all fuming when he arrived at the courtroom forty minutes late. His Honor demanded an explanation, and Alva told him about the geese, concluding with the words, "They were so beautiful I couldn't help myself. There are some things more important than court." The judge agreed—believe it or not.

When that child inside us surfaces, he brings with him a sense of wonder, a perspective about what's truly important, a wisdom—if you wish—about the good, the true, and the beautiful. And in that wonder, there is the freedom . . . to be alive.

I'm convinced today that "spiritual awakenings" have little to do with religion, or one's belief in a God. I've seen too many people from too wide a spectrum of beliefs (from Orthodox Jews and devout Christians of myriad denominations to committed atheists) experience in recovery a rebirth of wonder. I've a sneaking suspicion the "brand names" we give our spirit realities are far less important than the common core of our shared experience.

Keeping in mind that, as always, the opposite of everything is true, consider the millions who have died for brand-name religions—Jew, Catholic, Moslem, Protestant, Hindu. Have their "sacrifices" enhanced human connectedness and mercy, or has the "we versus they" denial structure been strengthened? Who can ever forget—or forgive—the "others" who martyred "one of us"? And think also of the ruthless "real world" where, to get along, compassion and mercy remain admirable theories that won't pay the rent or get one "ahead"—never mind that compassion and mercy may be all that really matter.

One day Alva and I had a discussion (as we're wont to do) about the things that are most important to us. We agreed—seriously, I believe—that we'd both be willing to give up our lives if the need arose. To date, though, we'd simply not found anything worth the price.

There's a saying around AA meetings that, with the advent of sobriety, there comes the realization that "there are no big deals." For years, that saying was offensive to me; it flew in the face of my idealism and self-righteous crusading spirit. Since I've had to accept my denial, however, since I've come more and more to choose living over dying, I've come to grudgingly concede the wisdom of that wisdom. Crusades do little but shed blood.

I've an uncle whom I admire as much as any person I've ever known. He's my assurance that there are healthy people on the earth. He's never been unable to cry or laugh. By all the measures we use to judge success—career, family, financial security, friends— he was a success. Then, in the space of a few numbing years, his younger son was killed in a plane crash, his son-in-law died of a heart attack, his older son divorced, and his wife (my favorite aunt) of over fifty years died without warning in her sleep. We all thought so many blows would kill him, but they did not. He lives today, more than able to grieve the loss of his loved ones, yet paradoxi- cally very much a man at peace, rich in love and humor.

I once asked his daughter (my cousin) how he did it. She replied she didn't know for sure, but that ". . . he [was] a man of deep faith who's just accepted, and accepted, and accepted." And one more thing, too, I think: There's a standing joke in the family that there're three ways to do anything—the right way, the wrong way, and Hugh's way. No matter how deeply he loves and cares (and he does both with the unique depth and fierceness of an Irish patri- arch), he's always his own person. I've had a number of wonderful father-surrogates over the years, but he's been my only hero.

I've a last story about Hugh. In the midst of those tragedies, he suffered a stroke. He went to Oregon and then on to Palm Springs for treatment and recuperation, returning to Alaska via Seattle sev- eral months later. While he was here, I got a call one day to let me know that he intended to learn how to drive once again, and that I'd been elected his instructor. I've seldom been so singularly hon- ored and scared at one and the same time. Luckily, the streets of Seattle weren't too busy that afternoon. He regained his confidence behind the wheel; I didn't shake too badly; and we both survived. A couple of years later, I remembered that afternoon as I began my own recovery. I remembered especially his humility and determi- nation to live—and maybe most of all his delight.

It made a difference. . . .

The opposite of everything is true: There are no big deals be- cause living is the biggest deal of all. The only real question is the depth and passion with which we'll embrace its gifts, or on the other hand, the niggardly defensiveness with which we'll control and fend off its offerings.

To conclude, Pushkin stalks catnip mice, bedevils Loki's and Princess's tails, firmly believes my fingers are his exclusive teething bones, and regularly meows his indignation and terror at being trapped in dresser drawers I've unwittingly closed behind him. Then he cuddles up beside me in bed at night to sleep in total, trusting relaxation. Each day he grows and comes more alive. He's not bad as a living metaphor for what that clumsy term *spiritual awakening* is about, for what it means to ". . . be aware of wonder."

Chapter 17

❖❖❖❖❖❖❖❖

SHIT HAPPENS . . . But So Does Recovery

Which Way Is "My Way"?

This past week I've had a potent reminder of why the Twelve Step programs tell me my recovery comes about only one day at a time. I've been trying to make arrangements through various banks for a loan. Since I'm still in the last stage of my transition from priesthood to life as a therapist on my own, my assets aren't substantial enough to qualify me for the amount I'm applying for. It's an exercise in frustration.

Besides, having to open up my personal affairs as one must in such a process is unnerving. I'm not the world's best financial manager by either inclination or training, so I'm convinced a priori that any bank person, upon witnessing my monetary bumblings, will laugh uproariously at the very idea of loaning me anything. That hasn't been the case. My credit seems to be okay; they like me and my future prospects; they've been as helpful as possible within their institutional guidelines. It's simply that the future isn't here yet; so for the time being, it seems, I have to go back to the drawing board.

Tuesday, after getting the same news from a third bank, my emotions rebelled against all that rejection. My back seized up, my stomach went into a knot, and I developed a migraine. From a rational, mature point of view, such a reaction is nonsensical. But for an alcoholic, codependent ACOA, it's the most logical of responses. For a day and a half, my body ached and the "Committee" inside my skull had a field day: I was worthless; I'd be in debtor's prison before Christmas; the "System" was against me; the world was hopeless; and I'd better commit suicide—or at least drink. Luckily, a good chiropractor, some bed rest, and a bit of reality-checking with friends in recovery snapped me out of my funk. Four days later, I'm pretty much back on even keel. Coincidentally, in the midst of all that Sturm and Drang, I marked my ninth AA birthday.

Therapeutically speaking, I could make a lot of analytical hay out of this emotional storm. As a person in recovery, though, the issues are simple and stark—with little need of interpretation. My dependencies are alive and powerful within me, and all these years spent in the process of healing are no guarantee that I'll be sober tomorrow.

That's not a thought that normally weighs heavy on my mind these days; it's not a constant worry. On the other hand, though, it's a realization that would be foolhardy for me to forget. My problem is not so much my dependencies as my *denial* about my dependencies. That riverbed, which has guided the flow of my life for so many of my years, has not disappeared—and probably won't until ten days after I'm dead. I'll not be so melodramatic as to claim that it's a beast of prey stalking my every footstep; but it is a constant companion, like the brownness of my eyes and the baldness of my scalp.

Besides the emotional imprintings all my dependencies have left on my psyche, my chemical dependency has left an indelible mark on my physical being as well. Like diabetes, chemical dependency does not go away just because it's in remission. If I don't take care of myself on a daily basis (choose to live in sobriety, practice "H-A-L-T," own my alcoholism, etc.), my chemical dependency will "go critical" once again with the same surety that day follows night.

So, add that chemical dependency denial to my ACOA issues, and you end up with a whole set of programmings that are almost eager for me to take any setbacks personally. Much as I consciously hate the thought, there's a large and powerful part of my being that still wants me to be a victim.

If nine years of observation and experience are to be believed, I must conclude I'm not alone. I've seen alcoholics with years of sobriety crossed up by the windfalls of chance and misfortune to suddenly find themselves drinking. I've seen codependents in recovery go suicidal when unexpected relational stresses buffet them. And I've seen ACOAs, after years of work, therapy, and Program, get caught in power struggles that have far more to do with their survival images and roles than their newly discovered and freshly embraced true selves.

I'm led to agree—much more by evidence than by desire—that addictive dependencies are chronic conditions. Furthermore, I'm forced to conclude that the chronic nature of our dependencies is, in the long run, the single hardest truth we face in recovery.

It's one thing for me to accept I'm ill; it's a far different thing to grasp, to live with, the realization that I'll always have my dependencies with me. Colds eventually go away; my cracked tooth could be replaced by a crown; my hernia could be sewn up; if need be, they could even replace my kidneys or my heart. But this stuff stays—hopefully in remission, yet ever alive and potentially virulent. If I have to go to a doctor, Lord help me if I don't share my truth with him before he writes me a prescription. If I meet somebody with whom I want to share my life, I'm literally begging for tragedy if I don't weigh—carefully and in depth—just how strongly my codependent and ACOA issues are affecting the ways I relate. Client after client asks me, "Doesn't this stuff ever go away? Am I *ever* going to be normal and healthy?" All I can respond with is, "I know your frustration. I often feel the same way."

My Life Is None of My Business.

Often I edge right up to the abyss of self-pity and despair (one way or another, come hell or high water, my head needs to make me a victim), but more often today something else happens. Thankfully, my friends and supports in recovery have drummed into my head—

and heart—a sense of gratitude. As I've mentioned· previously, everything in my life is new today; everything has changed. And it's all happened for no other reason than that I'm an addicted, alcoholic, codependent ACOA.

I've got no idea why my life—and Alva's, and Tom's, and Trish's—has gone like that. Some people might credit the roll of the evolutionary dice; others might blame a Higher Power with a perverted sense of humor. I really don't care which explanation may be right; whatever it is that's bringing about my life as it's happening today, I'm just flat bloody *amazed* at the results . . . and I want it to continue.

The evidence says it *will* continue to happen *if* I keep on doing what I'm doing. And as far as I can figure it out, what I'm doing is keeping out of my own way.

I'm discovering that creativity and growth are as much chronic conditions as chemical dependency, codependency, or ACOA programming. Writing this book has been a good example. I had no part in deciding whether or not I'd be invited to begin; I simply said yes when the opportunity was offered. I've been too busy seeing clients during the four-and-a-half days a week not blocked out for writing to think or worry too much about the next thing I was going to compose. I've just sat down with paper and pen at the times I've had available and . . . written. The book, like the rest of my recovery, has happened—sort of as if I'm nothing more than the conduit through which it flows.

Others tell me they've had the same experience. Whatever it is their recoveries and lives are about "simply happens"—when and to the extent they own their truth and take care of themselves.

Michelangelo could no more stop sculpting and painting than he could stop breathing. Winston Churchill could no more stop leading than he could stop thinking like an Englishman. If you read biographies of either of those two men, you can't escape their flaws and brokenness any more than you can ignore their greatness. What's more, you can't evade the strange fact that they both seemed to revel in their quirky differentness. What they did and were on such a heroic scale I find people in recovery doing in more ordinary dimensions. They become their own unique persons—slowly, painfully, resistingly—and wake up one day to discover that their lives have somehow transmuted themselves from dross to treasure.

It happens precisely *because* their dependencies are lifelong and chronic, for, very simply, if they were not chronic, we would not need to embark on a *continuing* process of honesty, creativity, and growth. Instead, we'd do as we do with most sicknesses: get diagnosed, take our cure, and then go on about our business as if nothing had happened.

When you're inside the frame, it's hard to see the picture. It's easy for me to see Alva's growth, or Trish's deepening, or Tom's quickening—and they mine. But ask any of us what we see ourselves doing on any given day, and (if we're feeling honest) you're liable to get the answer, "Same shit; different day."

You see, we're alcoholics—codependents—ACOAs. We're jaded, burned out, unable to be surprised by much of anything, not easily seduced by the enthusiasms of the world around us. Left to our own devices, we habitually expect boredom, betrayal, abandonment, failure, brokenness, abuse. Wouldn't you, if you'd been where we've been and done what we've done?

Yet I've seen Alva sit down in a mud puddle on a rainy day and kick his legs to splash the water like a delighted little child. I've seen Trish wear her beanie with propellers on top into oh-so-serious business meetings. I've seen Tom tickle a six-foot, two-hundred pound client in the middle of a stupendous rage. And I've experienced myself getting turned on by puppies and kittens and teddy bears even as I've slogged through the depressing swamp of my dependencies.

In other words, if our dependencies were not chronic, we wouldn't have time to grow little enough to once again become aware of wonder.

The opposite of everything—*every thing*—is true. The aspect of this disease that I resist most and have the greatest amount of lingering denial about—its chronic, lasting nature—is the ongoing source of my amazingly rich life today. It is the continual prod that keeps me living healthily in spite of myself. And when I do that— *in spite of myself*—very good things happen. As the Twelve-Step cliché says, "First things first."

The Joke's on Me.

A last note about my loan . . . last weekend, after my emotions and body calmed down, I got to thinking. I'd been approaching the banks as any rational, normal businessman would: submitting income-tax returns, property evaluations, statements of worth, etc. They, in turn, were doing what any rational, normal financial institution would do: evaluating my submittals and finding them lacking—not "bad," but lacking. But I am an alcoholic. So I decided to go to a friend in the Program who's well-off. I asked him to bet on me—precisely because I am who I am in recovery—and to cosign for me. He said he was interested, so we worked out an agreement and went down to his bank this morning. In the car, I was telling him of my excitement about finishing the book and about my busyness with all that was going on with my life. He smiled, but also said, "This is a great time in your life. But don't get so busy and go through it so fast that you end up with no memory of these days. Savor them. If you're supposed to have the loan, you will. If not, you'll be okay. 'Take time to smell the flowers.' "

So, besides writing today, I've taken time to play with Loki and think about the topsy-turvy wackiness of my life. If there is a "Ralph," He sure doesn't do things the way I would. I guess I'm glad of that. If He were content to direct me according to *my* urgings, I doubt that I would be able either to laugh or to cry today. Left with only my own addled understanding, I'd be so busy trying to defend, explain, juggle, and rationalize my dependencies (perfectly, of course), that I'd find no time for joy—or peace.

Coda
The Joke of It All

The Once and Future Child

This book has filled most of the unscheduled time in my life over the past year. It feels strange to be ending it. Naturally, I suppose—given who I am—its lacks and faults preoccupy me more at the moment than its accomplishment. But what's done is done.

Alva called me yesterday just to ask, "What *are* you doing? You haven't called in weeks!" All year long, Loki seemed to be asking the same question with those big brown eyes of his whenever I'd turn down his invitations to play in favor of writing another page.

What have I been doing? I get different answers from the different parts of me. The priest/theologian part tells me what I've been writing is a "theology" of sorts. After all, the scholars of the Middle Ages defined theology as "faith seeking understanding;" and what I'm doing is searching for an understanding of the belief system of denial, *the faith* that undergirds our lifestyles of addictive dependency.

The small but growing practical part of me that knows I'm responsible for my own financial well-being and security says I've been earning my living.

The addict/alcoholic/codependent/ACOA part tells me, as it has to, that somehow I've been trying to pull off a huge hoax, a con. People who'd take me seriously after really getting to know me

237

have to be bonkers, you know. So how could I possibly respect them?

The part of me in recovery says I've gone through a door that's opened, and that I should listen to the friends who say I have something to say that's worth saying.

Which or how many of those answers is true only time, readers' desires and tastes, and the surely surprising gift of tomorrow will tell. It's really none of my business anyway. Judging by the ease with which the words flowed, what I've written was ready to be written—and that's more than enough reason for writing them.

Yet, even though it feels "right" to conclude *The Opposite of Everything Is True* at this point, I cannot do so with any sense of final resolution. I still puzzle at all the paradoxes and questions raised or implied by the inquiry we've just explored.

I feel myself tugged in opposite directions by what seem to be unresolvably contradictory pressures. On the one hand, the more into recovery I get, the more pessimistic I become about things like society, causes, and communal justice. Even though our economy is booming right now and the Berlin Wall came down last week, I'm still unwilling to put much trust in the promises of any political leader. I'm more convinced than ever that the majority of issues that we get hot and bothered about—or even choose to die for— are ultimately hollow and not worth the spilling of our blood. The residue of abuse, power struggles, and, most of all, belief systems of denial—whether written large in the history of nations or small in the pain of individual families—is too obvious and potent to be ignored. I can't escape the conviction that the kind of work I do with people should not be necessary: If our world were half of what TV propaganda and politicians' blather say it is, I wouldn't be needed.

On the other hand, counterbalancing that pessimism, I experience a deepening hope. Channels of denial can be undermined in individual lives and in societies' structures. Maybe the Berlin Wall really has crumbled, in more ways than one. That I and others can earn our livings doing what we're doing says that there's a growing rush of people who want to change and recover. It could not have happened twenty years ago.

"The prospect of defeat was never a reason for not doing something worth doing," says Alva. Before the full sweep of the universe, it probably doesn't matter much if you and I are in recovery tomorrow; or if America's present "war on drugs" and Gorbachev's battle with endemic Soviet alcoholism succeed. It doesn't seem to matter much if we deal with the social issues, the greed and the prejudice and the lust for control, that give birth to widespread abuse, chemical dependency, and despair. Nonetheless, it does matter to me—today—that I'm sober and that I want to live instead of die. It does matter to me that I can be at peace in my acceptance and trust instead of rotting in my cynicism and stupor.

In short, I'm amazed at the contradictions and conflicts still alive and doing battle within me. I'm amazed that I can write as I have done, and believe passionately in what I have written, yet still be shaken and pummeled by the power of my brokenness. For example, as I was making my transition from priesthood to "civilian life," one person was of special help to me—Alice. She gave me support, and attention, and advice—all at a time in her life that was anything but peaceful and happy. Without her, I could not have landed on my feet as I did. In return, she asked for nothing but friendship.

A year or so ago, she remarried. She asked me to participate in the wedding. I was eager to do so: I laid out my best suit the night before and carefully prepared the readings she wanted me to present. I set two alarm clocks to make sure I got up on time. The next day, they went off, I got up and went about my day, not once remembering about the wedding until two hours after it was over.

My shame and embarrassment about that has kept me from contacting her since. Inside me there is still such a tremendous fear of being exposed as human and imperfect that I've literally been blocked from apologizing. I've been terrified of running into her. My kid has to do it right or disappear; there are no other options.

Until recently, I was so angry at my child's shame and fear that I could do a gut-wrenching depression just thinking about Alice. From an adult's viewpoint, my reaction has been crazy, especially since Alice is the kind of person who would be more than willing to forgive.

Nonetheless, the kid's still scared. I know enough, now, of my own history to understand why he feels the way he does. What's more, I'm gradually coming to an accepting compassion for his fear. I truly pray that, when I finally get to the point of loving him not in spite of his fear but because of it, I shall be able to reach out to Alice, too, with amends. Until then, I guess we'll both have to wait, and hope that time's passing will bring its own healing.

And so, for all of you who are secretly asking, "But will it all work out?" and "Isn't there going to be a happy ending?": Look at my own path to recovery as I've shared it with you here, and observe my experience with Alice. As always, the opposite of everything is true—in me and, I presume, in you. The title of the book is not an answer, but it is a truth that can offer us a new way to see our world and ourselves—a freshness of insight that can give, if not solutions, at least a gentle humor and the hope of rest.

Besides—finally!—if your kids want to play (and are half as impish as mine), every so often they'll tease you by whispering in your ear, "The opposite of everything *is* true . . . including this statement."